AF324275

SLADE'S WELLS FARGO COLT

JOSEPH ALFRED SLADE

SLADE'S WELLS FARGO COLT

(Historical Notes)

John B. McClernan

ILLUSTRATIONS BY J. P. KELLEY

Exposition Press
Hicksville, New York

Contents

FOREWORD 7

SLADE'S WELLS FARGO COLT 11
 The Gun 11
 Slade 13
 Washington Territory 14
 Eldorado County 16
NOTES 21
APPENDIX I 35
 Slade's Photograph 35
APPENDIX II 37
 The Military Record 37
APPENDIX III 45
 The Slade Estate File—An Interpretation 45

BIBLIOGRAPHY 65

INDEX 71

Foreword

This little book is not a history paper prepared in the correct, academic style. It is designed, however, to offer a few moments of entertainment to every history buff. Also, it carries an important lesson for antique collectors of all kinds. In this day and age folks who love antiques should be most careful in their purchases. This book illustrates how difficult it may be to authenticate an individual antique, how arduous the search may be to expose a fraudulent or counterfeit antique. Let the buyer beware!

Of special interest to the legal fraternity is the first, detailed review of the court records in the estate of Joseph A. Slade, written in simple, nontechnical language that every person will appreciate. This survey is correlated into the history of the Virginia City gold rush, its "Miners Government," pre-territorial and territorial records. Here will be found several new sidelights into Montana history, derived entirely from primary source materials.

The western historian will find here the most extensive bibliography yet assembled concerning the life of Joseph A. Slade. While he was a controversial figure in the early West, nobody can discount his contribution to the development of our country—in the transportation of passengers and supplies by the Overland stage coaches and freight lines, his efforts on behalf of national communications by Pony Express and telegraph, his rigorous suppression of outlaw activity on the main traveled highway to the West. He was the first premier of all western gunmen. An early Montana editor put it well:

So ended the career of one of the West's greatest gunmen. Joseph A. Slade, a man who had never robbed or stolen, who had risked his life many times that others might pass in safety—a man who had fought for his country and had spent the best years of his life taming a wilderness. Five years later another gunman, "Wild Bill" Hickok, who had gone down in history as a great peacemaker and marshal, was known as "the Slade of western Kansas."

> —WARREN N. REICHMAN,
> Editor and Publisher,
> *The Madisonian* (Anniversary Edition)
> Vol. 80, No. 38, May 29, 1953.

Slade's
Wells Fargo Colt

The Gun

This gun is a Colt Model 1861 Round Barreled Navy, 36 caliber, Serial Number 2833, also known as the "New Navy." It is regular in all respects except for an ingenious wedge locking device so mounted as to grip the thick end of the wedge.

The manufacture of the gun was finished at the Colt factory about August 1, 1861.[1] According to the Colt price list of January 1, 1861, the gun weighed 2 pounds 10 ounces and was for sale at $20.00.[2]

"For some reason the New Model Navy Pistol was never as popular as either the New Army or the Old Navy. Relatively few of them are found today in comparison with the other Colt Models," say Messers Haven and Belden.[3] Some possible explanation of this scarcity may be found in the work of a more recent Colt historian, who states, "Both the old model and the new model Navy pistols, regardless of their name, were popular with civilians, especially in the West. More pistols of Navy type have been found in California's Gold Country than all other Colt types put together."[4]

The Civil War had started April 12-13, 1861, with the firing on Fort Sumter, so it is not unreasonable to proceed on the assumption that as soon as the gun was finished, it left the Colt factory without delay. It is a civilian; there are no military markings. Today the back-strap is engraved "Eldorado County" and stamped "Depot 43." On the right flat side of the barrel directly above the wedge opening is a

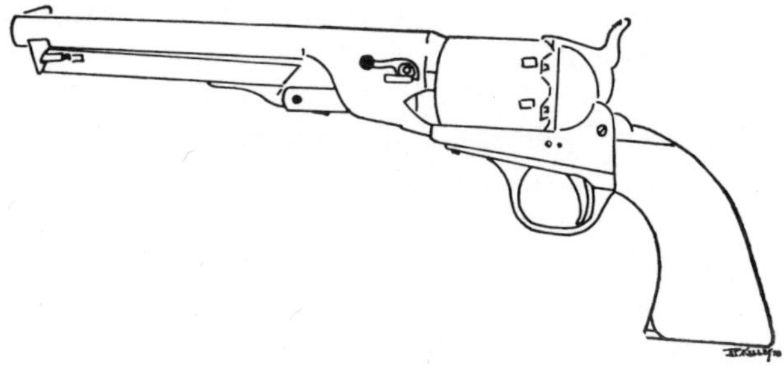

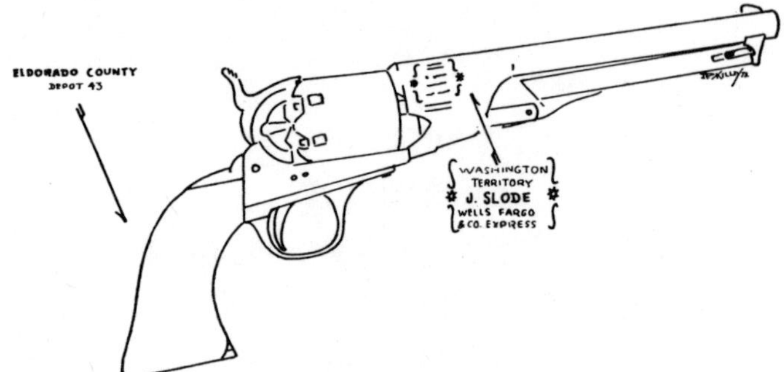

decorated engraving, "Washington Territory—J. Slode—Wells Fargo & Co. Express."

Antique gun collectors love to research a gun like this, mainly to vindicate their own judgment—to prove that the gun was a "sleeper"[5] and that they were wide awake. So your humble servant promptly commenced to pore through every available history of the early stagecoach lines, searching for the man named "Slode."

After several weeks of weary reading and when confidence was beginning to crack and crumble, there was still no evidence to be found that a man named Slode ever lived, much less was ever connected with anybody's stagecoach days. But finally in a recent history there was encountered the name of John Slode.[6] Eureka! Another gun collector went into orbit! The text roared out the message: Slode owned 134 shares of Wells Fargo & Co. stock; in 1866 his stock was voted at a Denver meeting to consolidate several stagecoach companies; he would be a charter member of the new Wells Fargo & Co. corporation formed that year by Act of the Legislature of the Territory of Colorado. What finer occasion could there be for Wells Fargo to present this engraved gun to John Slode? What gun collector was ever blessed with lovelier authentication for his Wells Fargo gun?

But a curious complication lay yet in store.

In the years 1861 and 1862 Washington Territory was a great, sprawling mass of land. From the west coast of the present state of Washington it extended east into the present state of Montana, jogged southward to the present state of Utah and eastward again into the present state of Wyoming. The searcher's only hope of finding out more about John Slode was to ascertain the whereabouts of his home town in this huge area known as "Washington Territory." With this innocent objective in view, an inquiry was made to the Wells Fargo Bank History Room, San Francisco, Irene Simpson Neasham, Director. After several weeks of painstaking and diligent effort by the Director and her staff the following facts were uncovered:

1. Early directories for Washington Territory do not list any "J. Slode"; the records of Wells Fargo employees of that period do not list a "J. Slode."
2. The typewritten notes of historian Loomis *do* list "J. Slode" and the name was transcribed into his book *Wells Fargo*; but
3. Old hand-written accounts of the period show that the owner of the 134 shares of stock voted at the 1866 Wells Fargo consolidation meeting was "J. Slade."[7]

Slade

Joseph Alfred Slade, variously known as Jack Slade, Capt. Slade, Slade of the Overland, etc., was born at Carlyle, Clinton County, Illinois, in 1830.[8] After a hitch in the Army during the Mexican War[9] he worked on the western frontier gaining experience in the freighting business and acquiring a wide reputation for toughness.

In 1859 Slade was employed by the Overland stage lines to bring peace and quiet to the stagecoach divisions stretching along the south border of present-day Wyoming.[10] This he did in the most effective way, with gun and rope, suppressing Indian predators and highway robbers in a manner which offered the miscreants neither time nor opportunity to reform into good citizens. All agree, outlaws came to fear Jack Slade more than they feared the Almighty.[11]

No sketch of Slade's life would be complete without some reference, however brief, to his terrible feud with Jules Beni, the founder of historic Julesburg, Colorado;[12] Jules caught Slade unarmed and unaware, emptied one or two revolvers into him plus one or two barrels of a shotgun; Slade managed to live through this ordeal[13] and swore vengeance against Jules; he eventually trapped Jules, tied him to a corral post and shot him to death by inches[14]; and finally he cut off Jules' ears and carried and displayed these dried ears until the day of his own death[15]. Mark Twain tells the story best of all, but there are hundreds of variations of it. However, all this gunplay took place in earlier years—before our Colt Navy #2833 could have come into Slade's hands—hence, it could not have seen action against Jules.

From April 3, 1860, until November 20, 1861, the Pony Express shared the facilities and protection of Slade's divisions equally with the Overland stagecoaches.[16] It was during this period that Mark Twain met Slade.[17] After the Civil War began with the firing on Fort Sumter April 12, 1861, Wells Fargo took over control, April 15, 1861, of the Pony Express until it was discontinued on November 20th.[18]

Thus, Jack Slade was indirectly doing yeoman's service for Wells Fargo & Co. for a period of seven months.[19]

About July or August of 1862 he took up residence in his new division headquarters at Virginia Dale station, on Highway 287 about four or five miles south of present-day Wyoming.[20] He had won all his battles with the outlaws and the Indians, only to lose the final victory to his appetite for liquor. He became a dangerous, drunken hell-raiser.[21] He was fired by Holladay during the last months of 1862.[22]

He and Mrs. Slade, and an Indian orphan boy who lived with them, moved to the Fort Bridger area, where he engaged in the freighting business on his own.[23] From there he followed the gold rush to Virginia City, Montana, arriving in June of 1863.[24] He remained a resident of the Virginia City vicinity from that time until he was hanged by the Montana Vigilantes on March 10, 1864,[25] at the age of thirty-four years.

Jack Slade was a man of scrupulous honesty, unflinching courage and herculean energy. Although he was reputed a gunman and was reported to have killed twenty-six men, he was never accused of murder or robbery, and was himself a member of the Montana Vigilantes.[26] Whiskey alone was his undoing.[27] Both he and his wife were expert with guns.[28] Mark Twain was familiar with all the gun models of that day and stated that Slade used Navy revolvers,[29] as did Mrs. Slade.[30] On the day of his death Mrs. Slade had rushed to the scene of the hanging with "Slade's Navy pistol."[31]

Although historians suggest that Jack Slade was penniless at the time of his death, the fact is that he left a substantial estate—two ranches in Montana's Madison County, mining interests, livestock, freighting equipment, an undisclosed amount of personal effects, and a personal loan of at least $1250.00 which was repaid to his estate. In addition we now learn that he owned 134 shares of Wells Fargo stock (at about $100.00 per share) standing in the name of J. Slade. Mrs. Slade, as his widow, became the legal owner of this stock, which was voted at the Denver meeting in November, 1866, when Wells Fargo absorbed certain other stage lines.[32] Two historians record the fact that Mrs. Slade, then separated from a second husband, was seen in Denver about that time.[33] She would surely have been allowed to attend the meeting and to vote the J. Slade stock, either in person or by proxy.

Washington Territory

Since the gun we are considering shows the address, Slade (or Slode), Washington Territory, it is appropriate to examine this phase of its possible history.

When it comes to gauging the actual boundaries of territories of the United States, the ordinary person is hopelessly baffled. Official territories were bounded by unlocated and unsurveyed lines of latitude and longitude, rivers, crests of mountain ranges, etc. It almost seems as if the early emigrant stood on the shore of the Mississippi at St. Joe and, facing westward, set things up by proclamation: just across the river was Nebraska Territory; further west was Utah Territory and California; southwest was Kansas, Texas, New Mexico and Arizona Territory; northwest was Oregon and Washington Territory; almost north was Dakota Territory:

> Before surveyors had an opportunity to lay down their carefully measured lines and boundaries, nature's boundaries were used to lay out divisions of land, both great and small.[34]

In the space of twenty years, 1848-1868, twelve huge territories were created,[35] and, as the process went on, each territory was changed, divided and subdivided ad infinitum. Four of these—Dakota, Nevada, Colorado and Idaho—were created in the two year period 1861-1863, which embraces the six or seventh-month residence of Slade in the Fort Bridger area. As of November 15, 1862, he had become jobless, moved from Virginia Dale station and set up his own freighting business.[36] On March 3, 1863, Idaho Territory was created. Slade left with the gold rush to Virginia City, Montana, *after* May 28, 1863, the date that gold was discovered, and arrived in Virginia City "in the spring of 1863," i.e., before June 21, 1863.[37]

Fort Bridger, now in the southwest corner of Wyoming, but formerly in the northeast corner of Utah Territory, was founded by Jim Bridger about 1842. It lies about 50 miles south of the 42° parallel and about 125 miles west of Bridger Pass, which was one of the points used by emigrants to cross the Continental Divide.[38] As a result of the Compromise of 1850, a congressional pact regarding slavery, Utah became a territory,[39] and Fort Bridger acquired an official address as being in Utah Territory. In 1859 Oregon became a state and Washington Territory was greatly enlarged,[40] extending southward to the 42° parallel and eastward to the summit of the Rocky Mountains in Wyoming, thus placing Fort Bridger about 50 miles from Washington Territory. Its official territorial address did not change until the creation of Wyoming Territory in 1868, although some historians thought it had been a part of Washington Territory and had become a part of Idaho Territory on March 3, 1863.[41]

This 42° of north latitude is the line of the north boundary of California, Nevada and Utah, and was also, at the time of Slade's residence in that vicinity, the most southern boundary of Washington

Territory. But as such it was only an imaginary line—a surveyor's astronomical calculation; it was not surveyed and marked by permanent, visible monuments on the land until the years 1868-69, 1871 and 1873.[42] The east boundary of this great stretch of Washington Territory was the "summit of the Rocky Mountains."[43] Fort Bridger, lying in Utah Territory but 50 miles below this unsurveyed and unmarked 42° parallel, was in truth an insignificant distance from the established dividing line of the future.

The people living at Fort Bridger from November of 1862 until March of 1863 must have known, as Mark Twain learned from the stagecoach driver, that South Pass was a crossing of the Continental Divide[44] and that they lived on the Washington Territory side of the mountains. What they could not have known was whether their settlement was actually north or south of that 42° of north latitude. Under these circumstances it is easy to imagine that these people, as well as their neighbors in other western territories, may have been in some confusion about the post office address at and about Fort Bridger. One historian says, "Such rapid changes in territorial boundaries and designations proved most bewildering to the early settlers. . . ."[45]

In any event, an order from Wells Fargo & Co. to a gun engraver to prepare a gun for presentation to a resident of the Fort Bridger area, giving his address as "Washington Territory" in late 1862 or early 1863, would not have sparked much of an argument, because who could have known the difference?[46]

Eldorado County

Depot 43

Eldorado County was centered in the gold country of California, extending westward from the shores of Lake Tahoe. Being one of the original twenty-seven counties into which California was divided, Eldorado was at first much larger. In later years it was divided and subdivided to make other counties. From 1852 onward it was the scene of Wells Fargo's earliest prosperity. After the gold rush days were over, Eldorado County still remained the hub of emigrant activities, in its role as the main inland route to Virginia City, Nevada, and the fabulous Comstock.

Of particular interest to our inquiry is the fact that one subdivision of the county took place in 1855 with the resultant change in Eldorado boundaries. In the next year, 1856, the county seat was moved from Coloma to Placerville (formerly "Hangtown").[47] We can easily see that such official changes were of primary concern to Wells Fargo, or any other transportation company, in order to insure accurate time-tables, accurate addressing and the publication of accurate advertising material.

In an early part of this article we referred to a recent history of the company entitled, *Wells Fargo* by Noel M. Loomis. In this work the author adopted a simple format which enabled him to include a vast amount of hitherto unpublished data. For instance, as a general rule he took one year of Wells Fargo history and made it into one chapter of his book, starting with the establishment of Wells Fargo & Co. in 1852. Again, in order that the reader might grasp the extent of Wells Fargo growth and development, author Loomis publishes two lists of all Wells Fargo agencies or stations and the names of Wells Fargo agents in existence in 1855 and 1856, these being the years of the changes in boundaries and county seat of Eldorado County. Then at the end of each subsequent chapter he advises the reader of new agencies or stations set up during the year, or those discontinued, as the case might be. It is evident from his text that the list of 1855 had proved to be incomplete and was swiftly replaced by an expanded and presumably corrected list of 1856. He specifically cautions us that there was no other master list by which deletions or changes could be checked.[48]

The lists are lists of so-called agencies; they are not referred to as depots. And this brings up the question of why the word "depot" appears on the backstrap of our gun. In every history available to this writer, concerning early western transportation, the places where stage-coaches stopped are called agencies, offices or stations; where the Pony Express was concerned, they are called relay stations. No western historian calls them depots, possibly because it is too trivial a matter to engage their attention. However, we have one item of shaky evidence still extant. In collections of Wells Fargo memorabilia we can see some indication that stagecoach stopping places were in fact called depots. There exists, for instance, a hat or cap badge (illustrated above): very old, authentic, concave, German silver, 3/32" thick, 2" high, 1½" wide, with the outside surface lettered, "Wells Fargo & Co.—Stage Depot." This relic of western stagecoach days seems to tell us that stage line agencies or stations were also popularly known as depots.

Assuming for a moment, nevertheless, that agencies, offices, stations and depots were the same thing, let us turn again to historian Loomis's corrected list of January, 1856.[49] If we give numbers to each of the agencies, which historian Loomis does *not* do, we find Depot 1 was Angel's Camp, C. G. Lake, agent. Depot 2 was Auburn, J. Q. Jackson, agent. Depot 3 was Benicia, Shirley & Co., agent—and so on through 59 agencies or depots. The number of interest to us, the number on the gun, is 43; and as we go down the list we find that Depot 43 was Placerville, W. H. Mansfield, agent. Placerville, which was already, or was about to become, the new county seat of Eldorado County!

None of us need to be told that the county seat is the place where county government operates; here is where the county board of supervisors meet to do the county business; here is where the sheriff and his deputies maintain their law enforcement headquarters. Here the department heads file with the county board of supervisors their requisitions for necessary supplies. From Placerville the Board of County Supervisors would have sent orders for supplies to all parts of the nation, including orders to gun factories or retailers for necessary weapons requisitioned by the sheriff of Eldorado County.

At this stage of our inquiry, with an abundance of horn-book history as background, we should be able to devise reasonable theories about the travels of this gun and its companions[50] one hundred years ago: such as, that the Colt factory sold the weapon to Eldorado County and delivered it with "Eldorado County" engraved on the backstrap; that the Eldorado people installed the wedge-locking device, stamped the backstrap with "Depot 43" for Placerville, and later on made the piece available to Wells Fargo for a second engraving and presentation to Joseph A. Slade. Indeed, many reasonable theories can be imagined to account for the markings on the gun, but we can't manipulate the actual evidence too freely in reconstructing events of one hundred years ago.

So far as the engraved address "Washington Territory" is concerned, the historian can live with this, because we know that Slade, for a short period of time, lived and worked in the Fort Bridger vicinity— very close to, if not within, Washington Territory. We could live with it, even though the Washington State Library at Olympia in its 1860 census, various directories and local histories, contains no record of a man named Slade or Slode during this era.

But the engraving of the name "Slode" instead of "Slade" is another matter. On the one hand, we can imagine that an engraver of the 1860s misread the name and made a natural mistake in spelling on the gun, just as historian Loomis did in writing his Wells Fargo history one hundred years later.[51] On the other hand, we face the possibility that an unscrupulous engraver of 1968-1970[52] forged the name "Slode" on the gun, using historian Loomis's book as a source, and by a one thousand to one chance picked the one name that was wrong!

Then we come to the use of the word "Depot" on the gun. While the hat badge illustrated here, referring to "Wells Fargo Stage Depot," has been authenticated by an expert antiquarian, yet we must take note of the fact that the antique market today is glutted with replica and fake Wells Fargo badges, buckles, etc., which necessarily puts our badge at least under suspicion; nor can we find anything in written history to confirm that Wells Fargo ever described its stations or agencies as depots. One prestigious historian[53] writing of that time and place mentions that Fort Bridger was not a depot for trade with the Indians. But for us to dream about our gun going first to an Eldorado County workshop, thence to a depot for trade to the Indians, thence to Wells Fargo for presentation to Slade, takes us to the very utmost limits of wild imagination.

Last but not least we must come to the bitterest medicine of all. If we imagine the natural thing, that the Colt factory sent out the gun with "Eldorado County" engraved on the backstrap, then that engraving could have but one legitimate meaning: that Eldorado County *owned* the gun first of all. So at this point we have to abandon history books and theories and get down to the nitty gritty—the actual, contemporaneous, written records. We cannot look to the Colt company for help, because their small arms factory and records were burned out during the Civil War, February 4, 1864, but we can still go to the written records of Eldorado County, California. County seat: Placerville.

The early records of the supervisors of Eldorado County, what business they took care of, what expenditures they made, are excellent —clearly written, precise and detailed. A thorough review of the minutes of their meetings during the years *1860, 1861* and *1862* discloses that at first the sheriff was employed on a fee basis, $1000.00 quarterly, and later on a straight salary of $333.33 per month; under sheriff, $150,00 per month; deputy sheriffs, $125.00 per month. Periodic, not regular monthly, expenditures were made for chains, handcuffs, repair and maintenance on a jail, blacksmithing and iron work; also, for clothes, soap, tobacco, tools and candles for county prisoners. Small payments were made occasionally to Wells Fargo for transporting county-owned gold dust or bullion.

But of greater significance is what these old records do *not* disclose.

During this critical three year period, so vital to the authenticity of our gun, we can be fairly sure from these records that Eldorado County spent not one dime to buy guns or ammunition, neither from the Colt company nor anybody else; that there was never any sale, transfer or donation by the county of any guns whatsoever to the Wells Fargo company; that the county never maintained any machine shop or depot, or employed any gunsmith or engraver who might alter, modify or improve things by installing a wedge-locking device on a cap and ball gun like our Colt #2833. In other words, the engraving of "Eldorado County" on the backstrap of this gun—the label of ownership—is false and counterfeit, because during these times Eldorado County never bought, and hence never owned, a single gun of any kind.

As the lawyers would size up the situation, we must conclude that, on the facts as we now know them, the preponderance of the evidence, that is, the greater weight of the evidence, condemns our Colt #2833 as a fake and a fraud. It was a fine and valuable antique gun until some weird scoundrel—scheming for a fantastic price—decorated it with forged and spurious markings.

We have good reasons to believe that Joseph A. Slade owned or used many guns: 1) The shotgun alleged to be at the Gettysburg museum; 2) The "six shooter" used to beat Jules to death; 3) The gun with one notch which inspired historian Birney to coin the derisive epithet, "One Notch Desperado"; 4) The pair of ivory-handled and silver-mounted Colts seized by Mrs. Slade from Administrator George Parker; 5) The Colt pistol used by Mrs. Slade to effect this seizure; 6) A derringer pointed by Slade at Judge Davis' head near the time of the hanging; and 7) A Joslyn rifle in Slade's possession at the time of his hanging, later presented to the Montana Historical Society.

We may still hope that authentic survivors, dredged up by dedicated members of the gun collecting fraternity, will eventually come to light.

Notes

1. *History of the Colt Revolver*, Haven and Belden, 1940, p. 100; and see serial number chart of Mr. John E. Parsons. Barrel wedges in cap and ball revolvers sometimes worked loose and were lost, thus rendering the gun inoperable.
2. *The Arms Collection of Colonel Colt* by R. L. Wilson, 1964, p. xxii. Our Colt navy #2833, all serial numbers matching, shows lots of wear and use. None of the original factory blue finish, varnish, or silver plating, remains, but the gun is not noticeably dented, scratched or pitted from rust. All markings and engravings are worn down but are still clearly visible. The rifling in the bore is also heavily worn but clearly perceptible, with very little of the pitting so common in cap and ball guns that were not thoroughly cleaned after each use. No sign of any fouling damage. Even the chambers of the cylinder remain in good, usable condition; possibly two of the nipples were replaced during the years of use. In short the gun has had a great deal of use but also good care; it was neither abused nor neglected. After more than 100 years it is still a handsome, functional piece.
3. Haven & Belden, p. 101.
4. *Colt Firearms* by James E. Serven, 5th ed., 1964, p. 134. For many years antique gun collectors thought that a certain, small, 31-caliber Colt pistol, which they called the "Wells Fargo" model, had been a sort of official side arm of Wells Fargo personnel. "Wells Fargo Colts" by George C. Chadwick, *Gun Report* magazine, December, 1957, p. 15. But deeper historical research proved this to be a myth. *Colt's Variations of the Old Model Pocket Pistol* by P. L. Shumaker, 1957, pp. 16, 17, 40. We now know the Colt factory in 1862 was swamped with military orders for 1851 and 1861 navies. "How the Navy Drifted Into Buying Navies," Paul S. Lederer, *The American Rifleman*, March, 1973, p. 30.
5. In the parlance of antique gun collectors a "sleeper" is an old gun of great but unrecognized historic merit, being exhibited for sale at a very cheap price, which is perceived and purchased by a smart collector, or is accidentally purchased by a stupid collector—to

the eventual dismay of the smart collectors. Sometimes the "sleeper" turns out to be a fake, to the regret of all right-thinking collectors.

6. *Wells Fargo* by Noel M. Loomis, 1968, p. 181.

7. Letter from Irene Simpson Neasham, former Director, Wells Fargo Bank History Room, San Francisco, California, dated January 29, 1971. See also notes 50 and 51.

8. "Joseph Alfred Slade: Killer or Victim?" by Lew L. Callaway, *Montana Magazine of History*, January, 1953, p. 5. *The Hanging of Bad Jack Slade* by Dabney Otis Collins, 1963, pp. 2, 19; *Vigilantes* by Hoffman Birney, 1929, p. 310. Birney says he was born in 1823 or 1824, and Slade in 1858 was "not far from 30 years old." *History of Wyoming*, Vol. 1, Coutant, 1899, p. 401. The military record, Appendix II, does not give the exact birthday, but in my opinion the data clearly indicates that Slade was born in 1830.

9. Callaway, pp. 6, 7; Collins, pp. 18, 19; Birney, p. 310. National Archives, Records of Soldiers of the Mexican War.

10. *Roughing It* by Mark Twain, p. 64; *Vigilante Days and Ways* by Nathaniel Pitt Langford, 1890, 1912 ed., p. 441; *Saga of Slade* by Don Prophet, 1958, p. 21; Collins, pp. 20, 21. Montana pioneer Louis R. Maillet described Slade as "division agent" in a meeting of July 2, 1859, the earliest firm date I have found as to his employment with the Overland. *Contributions, Historical Society of Montana, Vol. IV*, p. 215. For a curious mix-up of Slade names and Slade places see *The Bozeman Trail*, Hebard and Brininstool (1922), pp. 81, 90, 93.

11. *Vigilantes of Montana* by Thomas J. Dimsdale, 1865, 7th ed., p. 206. The stories of these killings are endless, but it is a matter of interest to note that Robert Spotswood, Slade's successor as Overland superintendent, kept his control over these stagecoach divisions by using Slade's same methods. *The Overland Stage to California* by Root and Connelly, index references to "Robert Spotswood." But Spotswood didn't drink!

12. Jules' widow stated about 1905 that the name was pronounced as though it were spelled Bené. Morton's *History of Nebraska, Vol. II*, pp. 180-1, Colorado State Historical Society, Denver, Colorado. But in 1907 he is called "Reni." *Story of the Outlaw*, Emerson Hough (1907), p. 147.

13. Montana pioneer James Boner stated in 1899 that he helped to nurse Slade back to health. *Alder Gulch Times*, 9/22/1899, Montana Historical Society, Helena, Montana.

14. Montana artist C. M. Russell made a pen and ink drawing of this cruel killing. To the best of the writer's knowledge this picture is

still in the Russell collection of the Amon Carter Museum, Fort Worth, Texas. The only account the writer has seen of the killing of Jules, given by an apparent participant and eye witness, was that of Montana pioneer Charles Higginbotham of Dillon, Montana. He mentions no shooting of guns but states;

This Frenchman named Jules was a squawman, and he was rustling Slade's horses and then selling them back to him. Being a squawman, he was in with the Indians around there and when the horses were turned out for feed they would run them off and cache them in the gullies. Then Jules would go to Slade and offer to find the horses for a reward, and when he got the money he'd send out and have the Indians bring them in.

Finally Slade got wise to the game and he roped this Frenchman and snubbed him up to a post in the corral and cut his ears off. I remember he cut off his right ear and put it in his right vest pocket and then his left ear and put it in his left vest pocket. He told the Frenchman that he would cut his heart out but it was so black that it wouldn't keep. He beat the Frenchman to death with the butt of his six-shooter and they dragged Jules out and buried him within ten feet of the corral fence. Then we all went over and had a drink." *The Anaconda Standard*, Anaconda, Montana, Part II, p. 1, June 20, 1920. For other exciting adventures of this pioneer see *Not in Precious Metals Alone*, Montana Historical Society (1976), p. 112.

15. One contemporary, without indicating that he knew about any feud between these men, spoke of the killing of Jules by Slade as a sort of frontier necessity and added another gory detail that has not been repeated so often, namely, that at the time of his demise Jules carried four dried ears of his own! *The Indian Wars of 1864* by Captain Eugene F. Ware, 1911, University of Nebraska Press, Lincoln, Nebraska, 1960, p. 180. In California cutting off ears was a common custom of that day. *Gold Rushes and Mining Camps,* Vardis Fisher (1968), p. 278 *et seq.* Montana pioneer, George A. Bruffey, who passed through Julesburg June 3, 1863, a "few months after" the killing, corroborates Captain Ware and others as to Jules's penchant for kidnapping other peoples' horses and returning them for ransom. *Eighty-one Years in the West,* George A. Bruffey (1925), p. 27. And see Appendix II.

16. *Wells Fargo* by Edward Hungerford, p. 76. *Ben Holladay The Stagecoach King* by James Vincent Frederick, pp. 56-60. Judge Callaway's reference (p. 9) to the Pony Express as the "forerunner of the stagecoaches from Independence west, . . ." was a slip of the pen. Judge Callaway really meant that the Pony Express was the forerunner of the telegraph line.

17. *Roughing It,* Mark Twain, Chap. X and XI. Mark Twain does not give any dates but we can determine from two things: first, the route he followed, and second, that he saw a Pony Express rider, that he met Slade between the dates mentioned. *The Dictionary of American Biography Vol. XVII* (1935), says Twain and Slade met in August, 1861, p. 203. The exact time and place of their meeting has been pinpointed to the morning of August 2, 1861, at Rocky Ridge—two stations east of South Pass. George R. Stewart, *The American West, Vol. V,* No.4, July, 1968, p. 11.

18. *U.S. West* by Beebe, p. 307. *The Pony Express,* Arthur Chapman (1932), p. 268 *Wells Fargo,* Noel M. Loomis, p. 155.

19. Beebe states, p. 87, that Slade was a Wells Fargo employee, but there seems to be no evidence to support this. When Slade employed the young Buffalo Bill Cody as a Pony Express rider, he did so on behalf of Russell, Majors and Waddell (Ben Holladay). *The Pony Express Goes Through* by Howard R. Driggs (1935), pp. 152-154. *Seventy Years on the Frontier* Alexander Majors, pp. 243 *et seq.* Chapman, p. 296. The record is quite clear that Slade himself was hired, or kept on, by Holladay and was fired by Holladay, Chapman, p. 270. Collins, pp. 21 and 34. However, it is also clear that, when the Pony Express came to an end, Wells Fargo may well have had good reason to present Slade a twenty

dollar gun in appreciation for his good offices on behalf of their company.

20. Frederick, pp. 95, 104.

21. Bancroft's *Works, Vol. XXXVI, Popular Tribunals, Vol. 1,* pp. 688-691; Collins, p. 33. *Rekindling Camp Fires,* Lewis F. Crawford, (1926), pp. 48-49. *Wild Men of the Wild West,* Edwin L. Sabin (1929), p. 169.

22. Frederick, p. 104; Collins, p. 34. The exact time of his firing can almost be fixed at November 15, 1862. Two Denver newspapers reported on what must have been Slade's last, big caper at Fort Halleck—the *Commonwealth* of November 13, 1862, and the *Miners Register* of November 14, 1862. Biographical file, Joseph Alfred (Jack Slade), State Historical Society of Colorado, State Museum Building, Denver, Colorado.

23. Prophet, p. 122; Collins, p. 35; Birney, p. 324. Of these three writers, only Mr. Prophet locates the Slades as actually residing in the town or settlement of Fort Bridger. His work is an historical novel, so his text cannot be considered solid evidence that the Slades lived in Fort Bridger itself. In fact, at this time Fort Bridger was a military reservation occupied by troops of the United States Army. In negotiations with General Albert Sidney Johnston we find that Jim Bridger had leased the fort to the government on November 18, 1857. See *Jim Bridger* by Stanley Vestal (1946), pp. 200-201; also, "Where the Deer and the Antelope Play" by Rowland L. Young, *American Bar Association Journal,* June, 1971, Vol. 57, pp. 577-579. In view of Slade's recent trouble with the army at Fort Halleck, resulting in his discharge from the Overland, it is hardly likely that he would settle down in the immediate neighborhood of military personnel. It seems more permissible to infer from Judge Callaway that the Slades had their abode near the Overland stage station of "Gilbert at the westerly end of the South Pass." (p. 8). James Boner of Montana said, "I was tending station at the three crossings of the Sweetwater. Henry Gilbert was at the station above mine . . ." *Alder Gulch Times,* 9/22/29, Slade file, Montana Historical Society Library, Helena, Montana. Boner was probably referring to Burnt Ranch at the main fork for Lander's Cut Off, at the summit of South Pass, just to the east of the Continental Divide. In 1859 it was known as "Gilbert's Trading Post"; in 1860-61, Gilbert evidently having moved westward into the Fort Bridger area, Burnt Ranch was known as the "Upper Sweetwater Pony Express Station." It was also called "South Pass Stage Station" at one time. See No. 5

Landers Cut Off, East Section and No. 3 (Parting of the Ways) of the series of historical maps published by the Wyoming Historical Department and State Archives (1959), Wyoming Historical Society, Cheyenne, Wyoming. Undoubtedly this station was one of several trading places of Henry S. Gilbert, a former station agent of the Overland, who engaged Slade to transport his (Gilbert's) property to Virginia City, Montana. (Callaway, p. 27). To confirm his various business locations consult the Gilbert biographies in Leeson's *History of Montana* (1885) p. 1268, and *Progressive Men of Montana,* p. 174. One historian stated after an interview with Mrs. Gilbert in later years that the two men were partners. "Vigilante Vengeance" by Arthur Chapman, *Elks Magazine,* August, 1927. Slade file, Montana Historical Society Library, Helena, Montana. If the Slades lived west of the Gilbert station, or anywhere in the northern reaches of Ham's Fork or Green River, then they were indeed not only inhabitants at Fort Bridger but also residents of Washington Territory, because they would be north of the 42° of north latitude and west of both the Continental Divide and the summit of the Rocky Mountains. In any case Slade was no stranger to the Fort Bridger area. Montana pioneer Granville Stuart recorded in his diary that J. A.

Slade killed a man at Ham's Fork of Green River in April, 1859. Birney, p. 319; Collins, pp. 19-20. Other historians report a similar incident in 1858 in the same neighborhood. *The Wagonmasters* by Henry Pickering Walker (1966) p. 81; "Freighting Across the Plains," Julie Beehrer Colyer, *Montana Magazine of Western History*, Vol. III, No. 4, (1962), p. 2. Mark Twain gives the story of this killing (p. 63) without comment, but Judge Callaway (pp. 19-20) doubts the truth of it. Another Montana pioneer, Louis R. Maillet, rode with Slade into Ham's Fork less than three months later, July 2, 1859, and made no mention of the homicide. See Note 10. However, the account of this affair is probably what came to the ears of Montana artist Charles M. Russell and inspired the picture "Laughed At For His Foolishness and Shot Dead by Slade." Slade was pictured by Mark Twain as an urbane gentleman but was painted by Russell as a murdering gunfighter. This painting was owned by Mr. Fred A. Rosenstock, art dealer, Denver, Colorado, and is reproduced as the frontispiece in Mr. Collins' little booklet on Slade. The picture of Slade killing Jules (See Note 14) has also been reproduced. *Book of the American West*, Jay Monaghan, (1963), p. 291.

24. Dimsdale, p. 196; Langford, p. 450; Collins, p. 35; Birney, p. 324. Yet Callaway, p. 27, says Slade got there late in September, but this conflicts with all the known facts—that Slade located and set up a horse ranch on the Madison river, built a stone house and a toll road in Slade Gulch, made a 1000-mile freighting trip to Milk River, etc. That he arrived in Virginia City in June is more consistent with all his activities, also with the biography of James Williams, Slade's reputed traveling companion (Callaway, pp. 25-26), who, according to Birney pp. 224-225, arrived at Bannack on June 20, 1863. See also *Society of Montana Pioneers* by Sanders (1899), p. 202. Gold had been discovered in Alder Gulch on May 28, 1863. *History of Montana* by Burlingame & Toole (1957), Vol. II, pp. 174-175. In his diary Henry Edgar sets the date as May 26; see diary quoted in *Shallow Diggins*, Jean Davis, (1963), p. 65. And the first wave of gold rushers got there June 6, 1863. *Forty Years on the Frontier* by Granville Stuart (1925), Vol. I, p. 262. A strict and literal reading of Langford, p. 454, places the time of his own near-fatal encounter with Slade as July, 1863. Whether the Slades left the Fort Bridger area ahead of the Gilberts, with the Gilberts, or after the Gilberts is pretty well settled. In my opinion the best and most reliable of the earlier Slade biographers was Mr. Arthur Chapman (already mentioned in Note 23), a pioneer journalist with the old *Denver Republican*

newspaper. After thorough and conscientious investigation he stated, "After leaving the Overland, Slade went to Fort Bridger, where he became acquainted with H. S. Gilbert, a trader. In 1863 when the news of the gold discoveries at Virginia City, Montana, excited the West, Slade took a wagon train to Virginia City, loaded with goods supplied by Gilbert, who followed later." "Slade of the Overland" by Arthur Chapman, *Union Pacific Magazine*, January, 1931. Leslie M. Lytle collection, Julesburg Museum, Julesburg, Colorado. There is no record of any reason why the Slades should have delayed their departure after getting the news of the gold strike at Virginia City, other than to load their freight wagons with Mr. Gilbert's goods. There was an easy route to Soda Springs, Fort Hall and Monida Pass, into Bannack and Virginia City. But the Gilberts could *not* leave in June; Mrs. Gilbert was expecting a baby, (William H. Gilbert, born Fort Bridger, August 12, 1863), and they did very well to arrive at Virginia City by September 1, 1863. James Boner traveled twice as far as the Slades and the Gilberts and still got to Virginia City in July, 1863. *Society of Montana Pioneers, Vol. 1,* 1899, edited by James U. Sanders, Secretary. (Madison County members). No evidence has been found to substantiate the idea that Slade "fled" to Montana in March of 1863 to avoid an arrest warrant from a Denver Court. "Afterthoughts on the Vigilantes" by J. W. Smurr, *Montana The Magazine of Western History,* Spring, 1958, p. 14, note 15. Professor Smurr quotes Forbes Parkhill, *The Law Goes West* (Denver: Sage Books, 1956), pp. 55-57. But we must consider the evidence to the contrary: First, indictments at periodic sessions of grand juries normally follow the alleged criminal event by several months, and Mr. Parkhill's entire text discloses that there were many such indictments by grand juries, with but few trials and convictions. See, for instance, p. 27. Second, contemporary newspaper accounts indicated that after the Fort Halleck affair Slade was released from jail on $2,000.00 bail after a writ of habeas corpus was issued by Chief Justice Hall of the Colorado Territorial Supreme Court. See Note 22 above. Third, Slade was fired after the Fort Halleck affair, and the man designated to replace him was Robert Spotswood of Denver. Spotswood stated that he went to Virginia Dale, spent several days settling company accounts with Slade; that Slade pointed out many horses, mules and freight wagons that were Slade's personal property, and that Slade told Spotswood that he (Slade) was going back into the freighting business. *History of Larimer County Colorado* by Ansel Watrous, 1911, p. 106. Copy at Pioneer Museum, Fort Collins, Colorado. See also, "Jack Slade, Mankiller" by Arthur Chapman, undated and unidentified magazine, Slade file, Montana Historical Society, Helena, Montana.

25. Callaway, pp. 30-31; Birney, pp. 309, 340; Collins, pp. 1, 48. Neither Dimsdale nor Langford gives the date of the execution. Other historians give wrong dates. See, for instance, Leeson's *History of Montana* (1885), p. 266. The probate file in the matter of the estate of J. A. Slade, deceased, in the records of the courthouse at Virginia City, Montana, leaves no room to doubt that Slade died on March 10, 1864.

26. Dimsdale, p. 197; Sabin, p. 170; Callaway, p. 31; Mark Twain, p. 74; Collins, p. 40; Langford, p. 458; *One Man's Montana*, by John K. Hutchens, 1964, p. 35. Bancroft states that there were more than 1000 Montana Vigilantes at this time. See note 21 above. Col. Sanders accused Slade of acts of drunken rowdyism but no murder, robbery or thievery. *Fifteen Thousand Miles by Stage*, Carrie Adell Strahorn, (1911), pp. 106-111.

27. Hutchens, p. 35 and "Slade of the Overland" by Chapman, note 24 above. For an account of his vicious, drunken activities just hours before his death see *X. Beidler: Vigilante* by Sanders & Bertsche, 1957, pp. 97 *et seq.* For those who prefer to classify Slade as a bad man see *Western Badmen* by Dorothy M. Johnson, 1970, pp. 43-52; or *History of Wyoming* by Coutant, Vol. I, pp. 401-406. Also, Watrous, who calls Slade a "desperado of the first water," p. 90 in history cited in note 24 above. Wayne Gard calls Slade a "noted thief" (Monaghan book, note 23 above, p. 304), but there is yet no evidence to support this. Certainly no responsible vigilante ever accused him of thievery; and equally certain is the fact that he was not hanged at Virginia City, Montana, for being a thief. Montana pioneer Robert P. Menefee of Bozeman said in 1899, " . . . he knew Slade several years prior to his coming here (Virginia City) and gives him a very good character outside of his periodical sprees, . . .", *The Madisonian*, Virginia City, Montana, Friday, September 1, 1899. An adopted member of the Crow Indian tribe of Montana (Thomas H. Leforge) spoke well of Slade: "The notorious Slade, two or three years later hanged by the vigilantes at Virginia City, Montana, was located at the North Platte bridge when we crossed there. He was agent for the mail-route and he was regarded as a very competent man for that position in those desperado days. IIe was courteous and helpful in his suggestions to the leaders of our train." *Memoirs of a White Crow Indian*, Thomas B. Marquis, 1928, 1974 ed., p. 9.

28. Langford, p. 456; Mark Twain, pp. 67, 69; Birney, pp. 323-324; Callaway, pp. 9, 15; Collins, p. 33. In the *Overland Stage to California* by Root and Connelly, p. 481, the authors state, "As a marksman with a Colt's navy revolver no one on the plains could surpass Slade, and few could equal him."

29. Mark Twain, pp. 5, 6, 25, 65, 67. In telling about how Slade cleared out a gang of thieves at the stagecoach station at Echo, Utah, it is stated, "Although a walking arsenal, he (Slade) was not a killer at heart and only shot in self-defense or for the company's protection." *Utah, A Guide to the State* by workers of the W.P.A., 1940, p. 357. Utah State Historical Society, Salt Lake City, Utah. In the Slade manuscript file in Montana there is very satisfactory proof that at the time of his hanging Slade was in possession of a long gun: a Joslyn rifle in 56 caliber, rim fire, which was presented later to the Historical Society of Montana. See handwritten letter, April, 1930, signed by M. W. Potter. In the Julesburg Museum there is a letter and a picture showing that as of May 6, 1963, another gun used by Slade had shown up and was in the Gettysburg, Pa., museum; it is a sawed-off 10 gauge shotgun; on the butt wood is stamped "Overland Stage Co."; under the forearm the number 518, and inside the forearm the name "Jack Slade." Slade had various nicknames, but historian Chapman records the fact that in his Julesburg days he was called "Jack." *The Pony Express*, Arthur Chapman (1932), p. 184.

30. *Footprints on the Frontier*. Saga of the La Ramie Region of Wyoming, by Virginia Cole Trenholm, Douglas Enterprise Co., Douglas, Wyoming, 1945, p. 71, quoting from the reminiscences of Elias W. Whitcomb, Horseshoe Creek, 1861, and referring to Mrs. Slade, " . . . She was forced to arm herself with a pistol, and going to the barrel of whiskey, upset it, threatening to shoot the first man who approached her. . . ." *Trail*, Vol. 14, No. 6, pp. 11-15, "Alfred Slade at Close Range" by E. W. Whitcomb, 1906, Colorado Historical Society library, Denver, Colorado. For further background on this incident see "Save Sibley" by Virginia Cole Trenholm, *Montana Magazine of Western History*, Vol. XII, No. 4, Autumn, 1962. This includes a picture of Slade by California artist Lea Franklin McCarty. For assessment of the work of this artist see McCarty article by Vivian A. Paladin, *Montana Magazine of Western History*, Vol. X, No. 3, Summer, 1960, p. 55. (With this article is a better reproduction of the Slade picture; a gun collector can determine that the revolver holstered on his hip is a Colt Model 1861 Round Barreled Navy.) One unknown contemporary claimed that Mrs. Slade herself had killed several

persons. *Banditti of the Rocky Mountains and Vigilance Committee in Idaho,* anonymous, 1865, with notes and bibliography by Jerome Peltier, reprint of 1964, pp. 142-3. And see Sabin, pp. 312, 313.

31. Collins, pp. 40, 42, 43; *Reminiscences of Alexander Toponce, Pioneer,* 1923, p. 152. Montana Historical Society Library, Helena, Montana. Here, in the manuscript file on Slade, is an unverified, typewritten memorandum reading as follows:

AFTER THE SLADE HANGING
*(Anecdote written by Mrs. Granville Stuart
perhaps from the reminiscences
of her husband, Granville Stuart.)*

Slade made no will and after his death, George B. Parker was named administrator of the estate and all of the property, real and personal, was turned over to him.

Among the personal effects was a pair of ivory-handled silver-mounted Colts revolvers. These Mrs. Slade claimed as her personal property and called at Parker's store to claim them.

Mr. Parker politely explained that the revolvers in question had been turned over to him as part of the Slade estate and that he would be held responsible for them and that he could not give them to her.

Mrs. Slade walked out of the store without comment but returned soon after and walking up to Mr. Parker said, "You say you cannot give me my revolvers, perhaps I can persuade you to change your mind." At this she presented the muzzle of a 45 Colts in his face. George took no time to reason with the lady but promptly handed her the revolvers which she coolly took possession of and left the store."

No effort has been made to trace the source of this anecdote. However, it has a strong ring of truth, even though the gun in the hand of Mrs. Slade in 1864 was more likely a Colt 1860 Army cap and ball in 44 caliber, rather than a "45 Colts" (a cartridge gun not introduced until the 1870s). The anecdote finds corroboration in parts of the Slade probate file. For instance, on April 14, 1864, a petition was written, signed and filed by Col. W. F. Sanders in which he swore an oath that Mrs. Slade was committing "waste" with the estate and was disposing of Slade's personal property to the detriment of creditors. On May 2, 1864, a court order, signed by T. C. Jones, Probate Judge, determined as a fact that Mrs. Slade had been "wasting" the estate "and has departed from said County taking with her property belonging to said estate. . . ." For further comment on this odd memo by Mrs. Stuart see Fisher, p. 318; also, see Appendix III.

32. Loomis, p. 181.

33. Collins, p. 46; Trenholm in "Save Sibley" article, note 30.

34. *Montana in the Making* by Newton Carl Abbott, 9th Ed., 1943, p. 200.

35. Oregon (1848), Utah (1850), Washington (1853), Kansas (1854), Nebraska (1854), North Dakota and South Dakota (1861), Nevada (1861), Colorado (1861), Idaho (1863), Montana (1864), and Wyoming (1868). *Messages and Papers of the Presidents,* Vols. XIX and XX.

36. See note 23. The Fort Bridger-Ham's Fork-Green River area would be a logical, central location for the freighting business in and out of Salt Lake, Denver and points in Wyoming. One early writer stated, "Slade next took up a ranch not far from Fort Bridger in western Wyoming, and began freighting." "Hanged for a Song" by Florabel Muir, *Liberty* magazine, June 30, 1928, Montana Historical Society library, Helena, Montana. If the Slades settled near Fort Bridger at the present town of Farson, Wyoming, they would have been in Washington Territory; would have had ample forage for their animals; would have had easy business contact with emigrant trains moving northwest to Oregon and places in Washington Territory, as well as those moving southwest along the Fort Bridger route to Utah and California. Additionally, if they received reasonably fast information of the gold discovery at Alder Gulch, they could move out with horses, mules and loaded freight wagons and, travelling by way of Soda Springs, arrive at Virginia City, Montana, within the time mentioned by Dimsdale-Langford, that is, prior to June 21, 1863.

37. See note 24 above.

38. *The American Peoples Encyclopedia,* entry "Jim Bridger" by Frederick E. Voelker, 1969, Vol. 3, p. 444.

39. *Short History of American Democracy,* John D. Hicks and George E. Mowry, 1956, pp. 293, 295.

40. Abbott, pp. 206, 208; *Boundaries of the United States and the Several States,* Geological Survey Bulletin 1212, 1966, by Franklin K. Van Zandt, p. 243 *et seq.*

41. *Pay Dirt,* Glenn Chesney Quiett, 1936, p. 231. *Montana the Magazine of Western History,* Vol. XX, Number Four, Autumn, 1970, p. 5. See also map, undated, "General Map of the North Pacific

States and Territories Belonging to the United States and of British Columbia extending from Lake Superior to the Pacific Ocean and between Latitude 39° and 53° North exhibiting Mail Routes, Gold Mines, and including the most recent surveys of the Topographical Bureau prepared by Captain John Mullan, Late Superintendent of Northern Pacific Military Wagon Road & Commissioner Northern Pacific Rail Road." Mullan built the military wagon road from Fort Benton, Montana, to Walla Walla, Washington, and participated in several surveying expeditions in the area from 1853 to 1862. *History of Montana* by Burlingame and Toole, pp. 55-58. See also note 46.

42. Van Zandt *op. cit.*, pp. 237, 238, 248, 251.

43. Van Zandt *op. cit.*, pp. 242-244.

44. Mark Twain, p. 86 *et seq.* Writers recount a story that when Slade was drunk he referred to himself as the "Bad Man From Bitter Creek." *Out West on the Overland Train,* Richard Reinhardt, 1967, p. 201. If there were any truth behind this unsavory nickname, if he actually lived in the Bitter Creek country, then he was still on the west (Washington Territory) side of the Continental Divide and even closer than Fort Bridger itself to the 42° parallel.

45. Birney, p. 12.

46. As late as 1900 a map was circulated in a popular atlas which showed Washington Territory as including not only Fort Bridger but also the whole west half of Colorado, far below the 42° parallel. *Cram's Unrivalled Family Atlas of the World, Indexed,* 1897, published by Geo. F. Cram, New York and Chicago, 1897, p. 207. However, it must be noted that literate and knowledgeable Mormon emigrants had long previously pinpointed and published the exact location of Fort Bridger at Latitude 41° 19′ 13″, Longitude 110° 5′, and Altitude 6,655 feet. *The Latter-Day Saints' Guide: . . . From Council Bluffs, to the Valley of the Great Salt Lake,* W. Clayton (1848), p. 17.

47. *History of California, 1860-1890,* Bancroft, Vol. 7, p. 439.

48. Loomis, p. 145.

49. Loomis, pp. 93-96.

50. Mr. Richard G. Bowman of Denver, Colorado, noted collector of guns and Wells Fargo memorabilia, writes, May 29, 1971, that *four* of these guns, similarly marked, showed up recently at antique gun shows in the southwest United States—along with collectors' talk that they had been unearthed from a warehouse in England. This information requires us to take into account the possibility that there may have been two or three other guns

involved in the same transactions with our Colt navy #2833—
that they stayed together, never being delivered by Wells Fargo
to the persons for whom they were intended.

Mr. Bowman adds, also, that a search through his excellent
collection of early Wells Fargo directories discloses no Wells
Fargo agent by the name of Slode—additional corroboration of
the information furnished by the Wells Fargo Bank History Room.
See, too, 1860 census of Washington Territory, various directories,
various Washington histories, which disclose no person named
Slode. State Library, Olympia, Washington, 5/15/72.

51. The name Slode is a rare one. No telephone directory west of
the Mississippi can be found that lists it. However, in a large
midwest city the name Joseph Slode does appear. On inquiry
Mrs. Slode, now 83 years of age, stated she knew of no member
of her family who was ever out West. Nor did she know of any
other family named Slode to whom inquiry could be made. Letter,
J. Garfield, Oct. 15, 1971.

52. 1968 is the date Mr. Loomis's book was published, and 1969 is
the year the writer first viewed this gun at Kalispell, Montana.
Whether a given specimen of engraving is genuinely old, or young
and artificially aged, is a question for an expert of experts. The
answer depends largely on the expertise of the forger, who may
be more expert than your expert! In a recent work we find the
following words of wisdom, " . . . There is a tremendous market
for firearms and their accoutrements; and, unfortunately, there is
an equally tremendous number of people piecing together old
odds and bits and 'improving' existing legitimate pieces with
engravings and false signatures. It has been said that if all of
'Pancho Villa's pistols' in private collections were assembled together, there would be enough to equip the whole Mexican
army. . . . Engraved powder horns and scrimshaw sell for quite
high prices by any standard. But remember, new whale's teeth
and cowhorns are easily purchased; and a good engraver with
no scruples can deliver almost any scene or map you want. Be
wary, . . . *The Care of Historical Collections*, Per E. Guldbeck,
1972, p. 39.

53. *Across the Wide Missouri*, Bernard De Voto, p. 378.

Appendix I

Slade's Photograph

This supposed picture of Slade—the frontispiece—has been done in pen and ink by artist J. P. Kelley of Kalispell, Montana. It has been published and republished hundreds of times since it first appeared in the late 1930s or early 1940s.

As near as this writer can learn, it first came to light at the Pioneer Museum, Fort Collins, Colorado. In a cheap portrait frame it carries the following inscription on the back:

JOSEPH ALFRED SLADE
Born in 1829
Died March 10, 1864
(Hanged by Vigilantes)
"Virginia Dale" Slade was good-looking,
dark complexion and less than average size;
weighing about 160 pounds.
Buried at Salt Lake City, Utah.
This picture given to Clyde Brown
by Mrs. G. L. Harris July 14, 1942

After careful examination an expert photographer stated that it was impossible to tell whether it is a picture, a picture of a picture, or even a picture of a touched-up charcoal drawing. Utah historians have referred to it politely as "this photo from an artist's conception of Slade . . ." (*Utah, A Guide to the State,* Utah State Historical Society, Salt Lake City, Utah, 1940). The most authentic evidence we have as to Slade's personal appearance is contained in his honorable discharge from the army—and the few words of description left to us by Mark Twain.

Nevertheless, in spite of its unknown origin, the picture is a handsome one, and all these years has been circulated and distributed to every lover of Western yarns.

Appendix II

The Military Record

Slade legends are frequent concerning his activities in the Mexican War. They mention his participation in the storming of Chapultepec, various other outstanding exploits, and even include the names (wrong) of his commanding officers. This is quite surprising, because even today the records in the National Archives, while not all we might wish, can give us a pretty good picture of Slade's military service, at least in broad outline.

Another legend, remarkably persistent, tells us how Slade, as a boy in 1842, had killed a man with a rock in Carlyle, Illinois, had fled to the West, had joined the army in Texas, and had been pursued for many years by an Illinois sheriff. His military record puts certain, logical time limitations on this particular homicide, and these limitations are predicated on the assumption that Joseph A. Slade was born at Carlyle, Illinois, in the year 1830. The reason that this is given as the year of his birth will appear later, when we look at his honorable discharge from the army after the Mexican War.

The Mexican War started May 13, 1846, and at the outset there were two regiments from Illinois—the First and Second Illinois Regiments, consisting of men who volunteered and enlisted for a period of twelve months. They were in several engagements against Mexican troops in the area of active warfare. However, when their twelve-month enlistment expired, they had had all they wanted of blood, sweat and tears and refused to reenlist. Consequently, the military commenced to recruit two new regiments in Illinois, composed of men who would be enlisted for the duration of the war with Mexico. "In June and August, 1847, the First and Second Illinois Regiments (twelve-month men) were replaced with 'for the war' regiments bearing the same names." (*The War with Mexico*, Justin H. Smith, 1919, Vol. II, p. 430.).

On May 4, 1847, Slade went to the recruiting people *in Carlyle*, joined for duty and enrolled for the duration of the war with Mexico, giving his age as eighteen and his occupation as a farmer. As soon as a full company was recruited, they marched fifty-five miles to Alton, Illinois, which was the place of rendezvous for all companies of the new regiment. Following their arrival in Alton on May 19, 1847, they were "mustered in", i.e., accepted into the service of the United States for the duration of the war with Mexico, on the 22nd day of May, 1847. Officially, Slade was a soldier of Captain Thomas Bond Company (A) in the First Regiment of Illinois Foot Volunteers, commanded by Colonel Edward W. B. Newby.

(Since we have talked about two Illinois towns that were no doubt very small in 1847—where everybody knew everything about everybody else—we can't help thinking it highly unlikely that Slade was a fugitive murderer as of this time.)

A few days' delay ensued while the organization awaited the arrival of other newly recruited companies from other Illinois towns, including at least one company from faraway Chicago. The "Field and Staff", i.e., the new regiment as a whole unit, was mustered in at Alton, Illinois, on June 8, 1847.

A regimental return of June, 1847, states, "Headquarters of Regiment Changed from Alton, Ill., to Fort Leavenworth in the Missouri Territory, as follows: Company A left Alton on the 19th June and arrived at Fort Leavenworth on the 24th June, 1847 . . ." The last company arrived at Fort Leavenworth from Alton on June 29, 1847.

Shortly thereafter the regiment started moving west on the Santa Fe trail. Muster roll reports were made out about every sixty days, and in early Company A muster rolls we find incontestable, documentary proof that, while "On the road from Fort Leavenworth to Santa Fe," Private Joseph A. Slade was "On extra daily duty since July 11th as a teamster." (See Company A Muster Roll dated August 31, 1847.).

What route the regiment pursued is not revealed, but we must assume that a military unit of regimental size—with horses and mules, supply wagons and other equipment—had to break up and follow roughly parallel paths, for reasons of water, forage and firewood. The August (and later) reports show only a few intermediate points along the way: Company C at Whetstone Springs; Companies B and D in camp near Socorro; Company F in camp at Cold Spring and near Limetad; Company H at Lower Cimerone Spring on route to Santa Fe, N.M.; Companies I and K at Cedar Spring, in camp near Secora, N.M.

A review of all muster rolls—individual, company and regimental—clearly indicates that the main body of the regiment reached its new station at Sante Fe in late August or early September of 1847. Hundreds of miles to the south the worst fighting of the Mexican War was suspended by an armistice, which lasted from August 24, 1847, to September 7, 1847. On September 8 came the battle of Molino del Rey; on September 13 the battle of Chapultepec and the seige of Puebla; on September 14, 1847, General Scott's forces occupied Mexico City, and for all practical purposes, from a soldier's point of view, the War with Mexico was ended.

In October Companies B, D, F, I and K marched south for El Paso, camping once near San Phillippe, N.M. In November they were under orders for the Lower Rio Del Norte and had camped once near Pulvidera; a month later they were at Socorro. By January, 1848, Companies E and H were at Las Vegas, N.M. In February, 1848— the month gold was discovered in California—Companies A and C met Company I at Albuquerque. Slade's Company A remained at Albuquerque until after June, 1848, when the regiment headed for home. It was back in Alton, Illinois, by October 16, 1848. We do not have the record of the casualties suffered by the regiment, nor the record of decorations awarded to any of its members.

From the military record thus far we can see that any personal and remarkable exploits by Slade must have been directed against local Indian marauders, because his army activity was confined to the supply lines on the Santa Fe Trail, and extended only a short distance southward toward the theatre of actual warfare. But like every private in every war, he rendered service that was just as important as combat for the ultimate success of the campaign. While on the Santa Fe Trail and in New Mexico young Slade must have heard many stories about the fabulous gold strike in California. Here, too, he served his apprenticeship in the freighting business, gaining the experience which in later years helped to speed stagecoach and Pony Express across the American continent. Here, also, he may have become acquainted with Alexander Majors, his future boss, who was in that area. (*Seventy Years on the Frontier*, Alexander Majors, pp. 74, 75 & 157; *Saddles and Spurs*, M. & R. Settle, p. 8).

On arrival in Alton the regiment was disbanded and the soldiers were "mustered out." In the National Archives we find Slade's original honorable discharge—rather unusual, because this document normally remains in the personal possession of the war veteran. It reads, in part, as follows:

Know Ye, that Joseph A. Slade, a Private of Captain T. Bond Company (A) First Regiment of Illinois Foot Volunteers, who was enrolled on the 22 day of May one thousand eight hundred and forty seven to serve during the War with Mexico, is hereby Hon-

orably Discharged from the service of the United States, this Sixteenth day of October, 1848, at Alton, Illinois, by reason of being
mustered out of the service on the expiration of his term.

Said Joseph A. Slade was born in Clinton Co in the State of
Illinois, is 18 years of age, 5 feet 6 inches high, dark complexion,
black eyes, light hair, and by occupation, when enlisted, a farmer.

Given at Alton, Illinois, this Sixteenth day of October, 1848.

This document, it is submitted, is rather convincing proof that
young Slade was eighteen years of age in 1848, had been born in
1830, and was thirty-four years of age when he was hanged in Virginia
City, Montana, in 1864. Young boys, anxious to join the Army in time
of war, have no scruples about misrepresenting their age—and, when
they look strong and sturdy, recruiters have never been prone to make
an issue over the age business. And that was undoubtedly what hap-
pened with Slade. On the other hand, when the war was over, and
it came time to take his pay and his honorable discharge, the young
soldier had no further reason to misrepresent his age. Consequently,
we may, with reasonable confidence, accept the age given in Slade's
honorable discharge as being true and correct.

So ended Slade's short and prosaic military career. He had marched
many miles, had put in many days of extra duty as a teamster, and
all without any black marks against his record. He went in as a Private
and came out as a Private; he was far too young, and in the Army
too short a time, to achieve any higher rank. (The title of Captain,
which Slade is said to have insisted on in later years, need not have
been a reference to military service; it may have been well earned
as a civilian commander of wagon trains.) Nevertheless, his volunteer
service in the war effort contributed to great results for the United
States of America: the Mexican War caused Mexico to give up all its
claims to Texas; and to cede to the United States all of California,
Nevada, Utah, Arizona, New Mexico, and parts of Colorado and
Wyoming—the size of this huge acquisition of territory being second
only to that of the Louisiana Purchase. (*The War With Mexico*, Justin
H. Smith, 1919, Vol. II, p. 241). It constituted 851,598 square miles,
or 545,012,720 acres, of a land which was popularly known as "New
Mexico" even before it actually became United States territory. (*Mes-
sages and Papers of the Presidents*, Vol. IV, 1841-1849, 1904 ed., Pres.
James K. Polk, pp. 634 and 493.)

Slade went back to his home town of Carlyle. On the back of his
honorable discharge was a printed form entitled "Oath of Identity,"
for use by the veteran in claiming his bounty land for his military
service. This form was filled in and signed by Slade on the thirty-first

day of October, 1848, and his signature acknowledged before a Justice of the Peace at Carlyle on November 3, 1848. Here is the earliest, and possibly the only, specimen of his signature still extant—and incontestable proof that he could read and write at the age of eighteen years.

This official action by Slade—appearing before a Justice of the Peace of Carlyle on November 3, 1848, to acknowledge his signature —again is not the act of a fugitive murderer. It is clearly disclosed as a voluntary appearance by a law-abiding citizen before a lawful public officer, for a lawful purpose, and the original public record of the transaction has been preserved in our National Archives for more than 100 years. It leaves us little historical basis for believing that in his "boyhood" Slade had murdered a man in Carlyle.

The honorable discharge and the oath of identity were sent to the appropriate authorities in Washington, D. C., with a request for the veteran's land warrant.

Prior to February 16, 1849, Slade talked to his stepfather, Elias P. Deming, about his plans for the immediate future and his desire to expedite the issuance of his land warrant. The substance of these conversations is preserved for us in the National Archives in a letter from the stepfather to the Honorable Robert Smith, a Member of Congress from Illinois:

Carlyle, Illinois
Feb. 16th 1849

My dear friend

In behalf of Alfred Slade, my stepson, I write you soliciting your aid in getting his Land Warrant. Slade was with the volunteers from this County in New Mexico. At an early day after his return home he made application for his Warrant. He is disposed to go to California and if possible wishes to get it previous to his departure which will be some time in the Month of April. If you can be of any service to him in procuring it at an early day you will not only confer a particular favor to him but add another to the many obligations I am already due you for the kind favors already conferred.

Your friend,
Elias P. Deming

Hon. Robt. Smith

The last shred of information in the National Archives is a brief notation, "Joseph A. Slade . . . Land—Admit to 160 acres—Warrant No. 50654—Issued 14th March 1849 and copy sent to Hon. Robt Smith, M.C."

We may safely assume that Congressman Smith was a good politician, that he wasted no time in forwarding this document to Mr. Deming for delivery to young Slade, and that Slade, therefore, was ready to leave for California in April as planned.

*　*　*

Did Slade go to California?

Various historical writers have commented on the circumstance that nothing is known of Slade's whereabouts from the time he left the Army in 1848 until he showed up in the Overland stagecoach service in 1859, but none have suggested that he was among the 49ers in the gold rush to California. Yet what would be more natural for this aggressive young man? To do what he planned to do? To do what he told his stepfather he intended to do, i.e., to leave for California in April?

In April, 1849, all along the Mississippi valley the wagon trains were assembling to start the biggest gold rush in American history. How can we believe that young Slade was not captivated by this gold fever? He had money in his pocket, a warrant for 160 acres of government land, and the whole mainstream of action was westward to California, to El Dorado county.

The index to the 1850 California Census (California Section, California State Library, Sacramento, California) discloses thirteen Slades in the gold country at that time (1850), with various given names and initials, ages and home states: Calaveras County—E. B. Slade, Edward G. Slade, J. Slade, J. B. Slade, Jas. B. Slade; El Dorado County—Geo. D. Slade, Geo. W. Slade, John M. Slade, Thos. P. Slade, Wm. Slade; Mariposa County—Isaac Slade, Jeremiah Slade; Sacramento County—Jno. W. Slade. Bearing in mind the wide range of guesswork, hearsay and human error which is known to exist in early census records, the candid historian will admit that any one of these Slades might be, in truth and in fact, the 20-year-old Joseph A. Slade of Carlyle, Illinois.

There are two further indications—in my opinion quite persuasive—that Slade went with the 49ers to California, as we know he planned, and that his California background covered a substantial period of time, probably beyond the year 1852.

Mark Twain tells a story of Slade killing three Indians, cutting their ears off, and sending them to the chief of the tribe—presumably as a warning to keep his warriors away from the stagecoaches. Judge Callaway comments on this story, along with the authenticated history of Slade cutting off Jule's ears, and expresses a suspicion about whether Slade had a "penchant" for cutting off peoples' ears. Assuming that Slade went to California with the 49ers, then this ear business can be readily explained. He would have arrived there about the same time as the mythical Joaquin Murieta, would have witnessed the ways that thieves and outlaws were treated in the California gold camps— one ear cut off for minor infractions, two ears cut off for more serious offenses—and could have decided in his own mind that this common California custom was an effective system for deterring bad actors.

Secondly, if he stayed in California for a substantial period of time, he may have observed the advent of the Wells Fargo company on the California scene in 1852. With the knowledge gained from his own freighting experience and personal observation of Wells Fargo methods, he may have concluded that the management and operation of Wells Fargo augered well for the future profits of Wells Fargo stockholders. Thus, we may have an explanation—admittedly speculative —of Slade's owning 134 shares of Wells Fargo stock at the time of his death.

However, more satisfactory proof of Slade's California connection, if any, must await the efforts of future historians. Maybe his land warrant will be uncovered in the archives at Sacramento; maybe Wells Fargo buffs will discover a long-lost company record concerning Joseph A. Slade.

NOTE: According to information received from the Bureau of Land Management in Sacramento, in those early days the new State of California did not honor federal land warrants, so the state would have no record of Slade's. The Federal people kept no record of the Land Warrant serial number; nor was there any alphabetical index by applicants' names until July 1, 1908. The only way to find the Land Warrant would be to know the legal description of the land involved— otherwise it would be a search for a needle in a haystack. (United States Department of the Interior, Bureau of Land Management, 2800 Cottage Way, Sacramento, California. Letter dated August 31, 1973.)

Appendix III

The Slade Estate File— An Interpretation

But in these days, when an effort is being made to establish the continuity of Western history, it is unfortunate that there is not more documentary evidence concerning such men as Slade.

"Slade of the Overland,"
Arthur Chapman, *Union Pacific Magazine*, January, 1931.

In recent years through the cooperation of the Montana Historical Society and Paul H. Love, long time Clerk of the District Court at Virginia City, Montana, the Society's library has added to its stock of historical material a microfilm copy of the court file in the estate of J. A. Slade, deceased. This file is quite bulky—about a pound of loose papers. In no sort of chronological order, it is all handwritten, in good and bad penmanship, on good and bad paper, often faded, worn and illegible; and, of course, done by lawyers in the proper legal and technical terms of the day. Although the microfilming process has improved the legibility, the overall situation renders the examination of the file very tedious and perhaps unintelligible to a layman historian. Nevertheless, Slade's estate file contains many items touching upon his own biography, as well as Montana history in general.

Joseph A. Slade died on March 10, 1864. Regardless of Montana's territorial status at that time "Miners Gulch Government" was in effect. (*Montana In the Making*, pp. 157 *et seq.*, and *Montana Government*, pp. 11 *et seq.*, by N. C. Abbott.) Abbott does not mention that a separate probate or estate court existed, but Henry N. Blake tells us that on June 9, 1863, the date of the filing of the first mining claims, an election was held and Dr. G. G. Bissel was elected first judge, Richard Todd first sheriff and Henry Edgar first recorder. (*Contributions* to the Historical Society of Montana, *Vol. II*, p. 87.)

In any event conditions were such that no great care was taken to preserve records of this type. We can easily see that the Slade estate file is not complete; in fact, we have the sworn statement of Wilbur F. Sanders that various papers had been lost or destroyed, due to the carelessness of the person acting as probate judge. Nor can we exclude the likelihood that in early years unauthorized persons may have rifled this file of valuable items for their own evil purposes. However, the volume of papers that has been preserved is large and is, it is submitted, rich in the stuff that interests the student of history.

Supplementing the estate file itself reference will also be made to certain records now preserved in the office of the Clerk and Recorder of Madison County at Virginia City, Montana. These records concern the period from May 26, 1863 (the discovery of gold in Alder Gulch) to May 26, 1864 (the date Montana became a territory), and constitute the surviving records of what Mr. Abbott called "Miners Gulch Government." Among these there is a book labeled "Book 'A' Probate Records," which appears to be a sort of court docket; it contains some fragmentary but important information on the step-by-step progress of the Slade estate from April 14, 1864, to October 31, 1864, but then ends abruptly. Unfortunately, the book of the Recorder of the Madison River District of Virginia City cannot be found. This book would have enabled us to pinpoint the times of Slade's claims on the Ravenswood and Spring Dale properties. There will also be a few references to other records of the Miners Gulch Government, as well as records of Montana Territory, where considered relevant to this personal interpretation.

The purpose of the law in seeing to it that a Court controls the administration or probate of a dead person's estate is to protect and preserve his property, to make sure that legitimate creditors of the dead person are paid out of that property, and that the balance goes to the heirs. Human nature being what it is, such matters cannot be handled by individuals privately, with any hope that just treatment will result for all concerned. However, there have always been many widows, then as now, who found it difficult to go along with these legal notions; and we can well imagine that, under all the circumstances of her husband's death, Mrs. Slade turned out to be an especially tough customer.

Specifically, we can see here at the outset that there must have been some high maneuvering—pulling and tugging—between Mrs. Slade, grief stricken over her husband and boiling with indignation toward the people who hanged him, and the various persons who claimed to be Slade's creditors and who wanted to know where their money was coming from. The date of death was March 10, 1864, and a month later, April 14, 1864, the Court proceedings erupted with a bang. Overall the estate was "pending," that is, being administered in the Probate Court, from April 14, 1864, to the final settlement and payments of October 27, 1866—a rather long time.

On this April 14, 1864, Mrs. Slade filed her paper in regular legal form entitled "Petition of Maria V. Slade," signed "M. V. Slade", and showing that Slade died March 10, 1864; that he left a will; that she was named executrix, with everything left to her; that Slade left no children or heirs, and that his property was worth $5,000.00.

On the same day Wilbur F. Sanders, on behalf of creditors Cook and Campbell, filed a petition showing that Slade died March 10, 1864; that he left a "large amount of personal property of the value of $5,000.00"; that he owed Cook and Campbell $200.00; that Mrs. Slade was committing "waste" and was disposing of the personal property without authority; and he asks for the Judge to order Mrs. Slade into Court.

On the same day the Judge signed two orders substantially the same, reciting that Slade had died March 10, 1864; that Mrs. Slade was neglecting to produce the will; and that the sheriff should serve a copy of the order on Mrs. Slade.

The docket indicates that on April 18th the Court sent out notices that there would be a hearing to prove the will on April 29, but that nobody showed up in Court on that day, either for or against Mrs. Slade's petition.

From these papers we can gather certain bits of historical data: we can reasonably conclude that Mrs. Slade's true name was "Maria Virginia", a name which has been changed around and garbled up in various accounts. From the papers and from what we know from Nebraska and Colorado, Wyoming and Montana, we can be sure she was the lawful wife of J. A. Slade, whether by ceremony with papers or by agreement at common law. The Indian boy, Jimmy, was *not* a legally adopted son, as has been asserted; and that Mrs. Slade estimated her husband's entire worth at $5,000.00, while Wilbur F. Sanders estimated Slade's "personal property" only (not including mining interests, ranches and ranch buildings) at $5,000.00. With her authentic signature before us, we may fairly assume that Mrs. Slade could also read.

We cannot conclude at this point that Slade actually wrote a will, because of later events in the estate proceedings.

At this juncture lawyers will agree that there was a most unusual situation: a surviving widow asking the Court for "Letters Testamentary" (her authority to take charge of all the business of the estate), and creditors accusing her at the same time of neglecting to do anything. Sander's petition could not have been inspired simply to force the commencement of proceedings, so that his clients could put in their $200.00 claim, because four other creditors had already filed claims against Slade's estate. (March 28, 1864; March 9(29?), 1864; March 30, 1864; April 2, 1864.)

In my opinion, based on more than 35 years experience in the administration of probate and estate affairs, Sander's petition was filed because he and his clients, Cook and Campbell, had reliable information from outside sources that Mrs. Slade was selling and converting to cash all of Slade's personal property—horses, mules, cattle, wagons, harness, guns, stocks and bonds, personal effects, etc.,—with the probable idea of ignoring the creditors, especially those who were saloon keepers or Vigilantes. Sanders undoubtedly suspected that she was about to leave the country with all of Slade's belongings, and leave Sander's clients holding the bag for $200.00. His use of the word "waste," in its broad legal sense, charged a multiude of sins to Mrs. Slade. Like many and many a widow before and after she seemed determined to take care of things in her own way, trusting neither to Courts, nor lawyers, nor judges.

The fact that the Court originally set Mrs. Slade's petition for a hearing on April 29, but that it did not occur on schedule, is in itself a trivial thing. In circumstances like these it is common for opposing lawyers to agree between themselves, for the mutual benefit of all clients, to postpone a hearing of this kind for a few days to allow each of them more time to prepare their cases. However, experienced attorneys will verify that trivial occurrences like this can easily lead to trouble. One or another of the clients may see no reason for such a delay, may feel that his lawyer has made a treacherous concession to the enemy, and may jump to the conclusion that he has been double-crossed; and the relationship of trust and confidence so necessary between attorney and client may break down completely. Thus, at this precise point we have a distinct possibility that the failure of both lawyers to go ahead with the hearing on April 29 may have been the last-straw circumstance which triggered Mrs. Slade's decision to abandon the probate proceedings and depart immediately for Salt Lake.

Proceeding along in chronological order to the next event of historical significance (but the reader will understand that we are skipping certain papers of less importance—claims, routine notices, etc.,—which will be mentioned later), we come to May 2, 1864. On this day a Petition for Letters of Administration—the legal authority of a person to take care of a decedent's estate when *no* will has been found—was filed by George B. Parker. He was a prominent and reputable merchant and first postmaster of Virginia City. He stated that Slade left $5,000.00 worth of property, horses, cattle, other personal property, ranches and mining claims; that Mrs. Slade had left the country; that she had committed "waste," and that there were many creditors.

Simultaneously, Probate Judge T. C. Jones appointed Parker as *Special* Administrator (to safeguard the Slade property until the Court could apoint a permanent administrator), after ascertaining that Mrs. Slade had been "wasting the property," and "has departed from said County taking with her property belonging to said estate. . . ." He then had Parker post a bond for $6000.00 and had a subpoena or summons issued for Mrs. Slade to be in Court May 6, 1864, and to produce Slade's will. Deputy Sheriff Neil Howie then certified that the paper to Mrs. Slade could not be served, because she could not be found in Madison County. (Deputy Sheriff Howie's certificate that Mrs. Slade could not be found in Madison County is not dated; but the docket shows that he received the paper, made his certificate, and returned it to the Court all on the same day, May 2, 1864.)

From these proceedings we can see that the preliminary appraisals of the amount and value of Slade's property were substantial, but more importantly we can determine with reasonable certainty that Mrs. Slade left the vicinity of Virginia City and the Ravenswood Ranch (near Ennis) less than sixty days after her husband's death. We know from other sources that she took the body south by stagecoach (*Rekindling Camp Fires*, Lewis F. Crawford, p. 48). He was buried in Salt Lake on July 20, 1864, under circumstances indicating that Mrs. Slade left the body there earlier and was not present at the time of actual interment. ("Slade of the Overland," Arthur Chapman, *Union Pacific Magazine*, January, 1931.). The estate file contains no evidence of a funeral bill.

The reader should keep in mind this May 2 date, and the name of the Probate Judge—T. C. Jones—because later on we must look at an out-of-court transaction of the next day, May 3, 1864, which was placed in the records of the Recorder of the Nevada mining district, as shown in the Miners Gulch Government books.

Soon afterwards, May 13, 1864, Mr. Parker appeared in Court and testified that he should be appointed as the permanent Administrator. In a display of most unusual diligence, the Probate Judge had his testimony written down into the docket and personally signed and sworn to by Mr. Parker. It is as follows:

George B. Parker was duly sworn and deposed that he knew J. A. Slade in his lifetime and that he died at Virginia City about the 10th of March last. That he has been informed and believes that he left a will at the time of his death, wherein he appointed his widow Maria V. Slade his executrix. That since the decease of said Slade his said widow has departed from Madison County and Idaho Territory taking said will with her as this deponent believes. That at the time of the death of said Slade he left property amounting to between $7000 & $8000. That Maria V. Slade took away with her a large amount of personal property and deponent believes that the property left in said county will not exceed in value $4000. That the debts outstanding against said estate will as deponent believes exceed the value of the property now left in said county belonging to said estate. Deponent further saith that he does not know where said Maria V. Slade now is, nor the names or places of residence of any of said Slade's relatives.

/s/ G. B. Parker

Subscribed & sworn before
me this 13th day of May, 1864

T. C. Jones
Probate Judge

Thereupon, George B. Parker was appointed regular administrator, but the Probate Judge, presumably knowing of more property, required him to furnish an even bigger bond—$8,000.00. His bondsmen were John A. Creighton and E. C. Mason. Such a bond would reflect only the value of personal property; it would not include real property like ranches, the law recognizing that nobody can pick up a ranch and run away with it.

On July 20, 1864, Administrator Parker leased the Ravenswood Ranch to Thomas F. Phillips for five months in order to harvest the hay. This ranch was in the Madison Valley between McAllister and Ennis. In the office of the U. S. Bureau of Land Management at Billings, Montana, there is an old notation on the original survey plat of Township 5 South, Range 1 West, Montana Principal Meridian, showing that the South Half of Section 10 was "Slades Claim."

On July 23, 1864, Administrator Parker filed his first "inventory and appraisement" of the Slade estate disclosing that it included the Ravenswood Ranch, estimated at $2,000.00, and the Spring Dale ranch, estimated at $250.00. Another asset appears for the first time: a promissory note for $1250.00 due to Slade from Baume and Southmayd, secured by a mortgage on mining claims in the Nevada mining district. This promise to pay by Baume and Southmayd is erroneously referred to as being dated March 12, 1864—two days after Slade's death—and it called for Baume and Southmayd to repay the money to Slade on

July 1, 1864. Administrator Parker collected the full amount of this note for the benefit of the Slade estate, although he had to start a lawsuit in order to force payment.

This Baume and Southmayd note presents a mystery, indeed. If we digress a while from the Slade estate file and look into the contemporary Miners Gulch Government records, we come upon information both enlightening and baffling.

Remembering that on May 2, 1864, Probate Judge T. C. Jones, after determining that Mrs. Slade was gone from Virginia City, had placed George Parker in charge of Slade's property as Special Administrator, we now discover a strange transaction. The next day, May 3, 1864, a mortgage was made. On page 77 of Record Book B of the Nevada District, Idaho Territory, (later filed with the appropriate officer of the new Montana Territory on July 11, 1870.), claims 5 and 6 in that district were mortgaged with the following language included:

> The said Leroy Southmayd & Amos C. Hall are to make the following payments one thousand dollars in hand also two notes of 2750 twenty seven hundred and fifty dollars held by Mrs J. A. Slade and Thomas Jones also one note held by S Southmayd and Co of two hundred and Ninty dollars also note held Thomas Morris of six hundred . . . .

/s/ C W Southmayd

Thomas Baume
May 3, 1864

In presents of
Jas. L. Middaugh
W. N. Lutts

filed May 4, 1864
M H Lott *Recorder*
J W Nighwander *Deputy*

On the following day, May 4, 1864, Leroy Southmayd deeded his interest in claims 5 and 6 to C. W. Southmayd for $4640.00 (Page 76 of the same book.).

On July 5, 1864, C. W. Southmayd then deeded his interest in claims 5 and 6 to West and Dickason for $2500.00 in the following picturesque language (Page 176 of the same book):

Nevada July 5, 1864

> Know all men by these presents that I C. W. Southmayd has this day sold West & Dickason all mi rite title and interest in Claims No five and six on Mahers Bar Below None as the Slade and Jones Claims for the sum of 25 hundred dollars in hand paid

                                              /s/ C W Southmayd

                                  Filed for record July 5, 1864
Witness   M H Lott   Recorder
J W Beam   Nighwander   Deputy

On July 13, 1864, we have seen that George Parker was appointed regular Administrator, and on July 23, 1864, he inventories and reports to the Court a misdated Baume and Southmayd note for $1250.00.

In viewing these strange goings on we must not lose our faith in human nature, but we must concede that the cold, official, written record certainly indicates a conspiracy on foot to pilfer and defraud the Slade estate. The loss to the estate would be $2750.00 less $1250.00, or $1500.00 plus substantial interest. (Some loans at Virginia City were made at an interest rate of 10% per month!)

If the Probate Judge, T. C. Jones, was the same man as the Thomas Jones mentioned in the mortgage, or a close relative, then the finger of suspicion would have to point at him as one of the main villains in this out-of-court fancy work. He had knowledge that the estate would be administered, that Mrs. Slade was gone, and that he himself had a substantial interest to protect by having it recorded. A second finger of suspicion would have to point, of course, at C. W. Southmayd and Thomas Baume, since they stood to gain an immediate profit by forging and substituting a new note. All guilty participants must have relied on the assumption that Mrs. Slade had lost, or overlooked, the original note among Slade's effects. Anyway, we can rest assured that not all frontier robberies were confined to stagecoaches or gambling dens. Little wonder that we find Administrator Parker the following year denouncing and condemning the operations of the Probate Court in Virginia City. (See his Motion dated October 25, 1868 [error?] and his Report dated November 7, 1865.). Twenty years later Wilbur F. Sanders singled out and praised five pioneer Montana judges—but he had no kind word for brother Jones. (*Reports of Montana Bar Association, Vol. I, 1885 to 1902*, p. 170.).

By this time in our study of the Slade estate file the reader will agree that, while Slade may have owed a lot of bills on the day of his death, he could not be described as "penniless" or broke, as some historians have declared. Also, we see that Slade was not merely a drunken hell-raiser but was in fact a substantial investor in the Virginia City mining industry.

If we disregard the motivation prompting the Baume and Southmayd transaction, we learn still more about Slade, who has been described as strictly a freighter. He and Jones each put up $2750.00 to develop these claims, which were certainly rich ones if the monies involved mean anything. We cannot say for sure, but in this situation the original promissory note, i.e., the loan, must have been for at least six months or a year; in other words, the loan to Baume and Southmayd must have been made by Slade a substantial time before his death. The investment in the claims was so heavy that people generally in the Virginia City area, for some period of months, thought Slade and Jones owned this mine; otherwise why would Southmayd himself on July 5, 1864—four months after Slade's death—make his deed referring to the property as the "Slade and Jones" claims?

In addition to the "Slade and Jones" venture there is fragmentary and inconclusive evidence that Slade himself, or some friend on his behalf, staked out a couple of mining claims in the Granite Gulch mining district-one of them as of November 17, 1863. These were the "Lone Tree" and the "Mormon Boy." The name of the locator is garbled but it appears to be "A. J." Slade. (See Granite Gulch Records, index of claims on Mill Bar under A. J. Slade; Granite Gulch Records, page 16, entry dated November 17, 1863; unlabeled book with pencil entry back of front cover, "2nd Index to ter. Records of Madison Co. to pre-emptions . . ." page 315, entry dated February 4, 1865.). I could find no record actually linking these claims with our man J. A. Slade— nor any record of an A. J. Slade being in the neighborhood at that time and place. The reader will note, however, that these claims were not included in Administrator Parker's inventory of J. A. Slade's estate.

On September 7, 1864, Administrator Parker filed a Petition to sell Slade's personal property and real estate in order to pay off debts estimated at $4000.00 or $5000.00. For the first time we see mentioned the fact Slade's estate included a herd of dairy cows, but that they were then involved in a law suit. This bit of information would tend to corroborate various historical narratives to the effect that the Slades sold milk in the Virginia City area.

If we make a chronological jump to an account filed November 7, 1865, we can see these dairy herd cattle mentioned at a value of $3000.00, and the law suit identified as "M. Domis v. Administrator Parker." Possibly Slade had just acquired this dairy herd on a down payment of $3000.00. When the seller heard of the hanging, he may have started the law suit against Administrator Parker in order to repossess the animals. This is only a guess, because I have not been able to locate the court file of this case to confirm what it was about. In any event Administrator Parker participated in the law suit. As of his first accounting, November 7, 1865, it was "not yet collected," but the final accounting and settlement, dated the same day, indicates the $3000.00 *was* returned to Administrator Parker and the cattle returned to the seller, i.e., the law suit evidently came to an end by agreement between the parties.

October 24, 1864. At this point we will look briefly at one of the claims against the estate, because it gives us an idea of how some of the estate business was handled. This is a claim for $1503.25 by George Parker, the administrator himself, and was in addition to another claim of his own for $554.32 for goods purchased from his store by the Slades. This $1503.25 claim by the administrator was alleged to have been filed October 24, 1864, then lost or destroyed by the Probate Judge, and then subsequently replaced with a copy in the file on November 7, 1865. While it is dated July, 1864, it appears to be an itemization of monies paid out by the Administrator from the time he first took over the management of the estate, May 2, 1864, until July of 1864; all of which is added up to a total of $1503.25 and placed as a claim against the estate, so that Administrator Parker could be reimbursed for these expenditures.

This claim, showing amounts advanced by the Administrator out of his own pocket, may be summarized as follows:

July 1864 to:	*Oz.*	*Dwts.*	*Grs.*	*Approx.*
Mrs. Slade	5	11	3	$200.00
W. J. Norris	4	3	15	150.00
J.J. Root Co.	4	8	21	165.00
Higgins & Thorne	1	17	6	65.00
W. W. Brown	3	14	4	130.00
Griffith & Thompson	4	5	13	160.00
Creighton & Co.	13	7	9	465.00
Mrs. Slade	5	11	3	200.00
				$1535.00

(Using 24 grains gold=1 pennyweight (DWT); 20 pennyweights =1 ounce; 1 ounce=$35.00.)

The presence of this claim indicates that from time to time people with legitimate claims against Slade's estate would go to Mr. Parker's store—possibly hard pressed for money, or about to leave the territory —and Administrator Parker would advance his own money to pay off their claim, knowing, of course, that there were ample assets in the estate to repay himself. This probably seemed to be a common sense way of doing things rather than making a deserving creditor wait until the final settlement of all the affairs of the estate; but today it would be considered highly irregular, a course of conduct likely to lead to financial mistakes or fraud.

As pointed out, while the claim is merely dated "July, 1864," it is likely that July was simply the month when the account was recapitulated and put into claim form. The advances by Administrator Parker were undoubtedly made over the longer period of time, from May 2, 1864, to July, 1864. Most interesting to us is the fact that Administrator Parker made two separate but identical advances of funds to the widow, Mrs. Slade, giving her gold dust on each occasion in the amount of 5 ounces, 11 penneyweights and 3 grains, or approximately $200.00 (figuring gold at $35 per ounce). Yet, there may be a minor discrepancy here. We have seen that Neil Howie, Deputy Sheriff, certified that Mrs. Slade was gone from Madison County on May 2, 1864. Possibly Mr. Parker advanced the first $200.00 a day or so before May 2, to take care of her travel expense, and then made the second advance by some sort of mail order arrangement.

The claims of W. J. Norris ($150.00), J. J. Root Co. ($165.00), Higgins & Thorne ($65.00), W. W. Brown ($130.00), Griffith & Thompson ($160.00) and Creighton & Co. ($465.00) cannot be scrutinized, because these claims were evidently among the papers lost or destroyed; and on the final settlement of the estate there was no point for these creditors to file another copy, because they had already been paid by Administrator Parker at his store. However, we *are* able to scrutinize the first account and the final settlement (both filed November 7, 1865), and the candid observer must admit to a suspicion that some of these creditors, or maybe somebody else, received double payment from the Slade estate—once at Administrator Parker's store and again on the final settlement of the estate—an inevitable occurrence whenever an administrator advances money out of his own funds to take care of estate business.

Be that as it may, the historian can clearly see that Administrator Parker, an able and capable business man at Virginia City, knew from the outset that Slade was not broke, that he owned ample property to take care of any and all legitimate debts.

The two ranches were sold at public auction on December 19, 1864. John R. Rockfellow got the 320-acre Ravenswood ranch on a bid of $500.00, and Benjamin F. Christenot got the 160-acre Spring Dale ranch on a bid of $105.00. Rockfellow also got all available hay at $12.00 per ton (see administrator's and auctioneer's reports of December 31, 1864). One freight wagon, horse collars, harness, wagon wheels and a worn-out bay mare brought $176.75, which, together with the hay, came to a total of $391.79.

On January 25, 1865, the Probate Court approved the sales and ordered Administrator Parker to deliver deeds for the two ranches to the purchasers. These appear in the records of the County Clerk and Recorder of Madison County in Book F of Deeds, page 45 (for the Ravenswood ranch) and Book R of Deeds, page 23 (for the Spring Dale ranch).

At this point in the chronology of the estate affairs the situation becomes hopelessly confused. We can reasonably infer, however, that from about November of 1864 until the end of January, 1865, whoever was acting as Probate Judge had failed to do his duties—many papers had been lost or destroyed. Outraged at this turn of events, and filing copies of the lost papers were: Wilbur F. Sanders as attorney for creditors James Boner and James H. Williams (papers filed January 25, 1865); Wilbur F. Sanders again, as attorney for creditor J. J. Hall (paper filed October 6 or 11, 1865); G. E. Kettle, creditor (paper filed October 18, 1865); and Administrator Parker himself charging the Probate Judge with "gross negligence" (paper appearing to be dated October 25, 1868, but undoubtedly intended to be October 25, 1865, and Administrator's report of Nov. 7, 1865). Some of this confusion may be explained by outside circumstances: On May 26, 1864, Montana had become a Territory; in the Fall of 1864 the first territorial government was organizing at Bannack; on March 22, 1865, Mrs. Slade was back in Virginia City and was married to Kiskadden; on April 5, 1865, Rockfellow deeded the Ravenwood ranch back to Mrs. "Slade" for $850.00 (Book F of Deeds, p. 430, county records mentioned above).

As mentioned before, on November 7, 1865, Administrator Parker filed his "first account" showing cash on hand in the amount of $2,246.79, and a credit of $3000.00 for the dairy herd involved in the lawsuit. The mention in this first account of "cattle" must necessarily refer to the dairy herd, because the administrator and the auctioneer had already sold all of Slade's personal property on December 19, 1864. Since the size of the auctioneer's commission—see item appearing to be dated December 31, 1864, claim of George Higgins, auctioneer— depended on the total amount realized, we can safely assume that he sold everything possible, except the cattle involved in the lawsuit.

Up to this time the expenses of administration had mounted up to $968.24.

The same day, November 7, 1865, Administrator Parker also filed his *final* account for "Final Settlement." This final settlement mentions nothing about "cattle" but treats the $3000.00, "not yet collected" as per the first account, as cash on hand; and hence we can conclude that the $3000.00 was paid into the estate, the cattle were returned to the seller, and the lawsuit was settled, all on the same day. Certainly

Administrator Parker would not account and be responsible for that sum of money unless he had it on hand.

The final settlement covers all payments made to general creditors of the estate, plus some additional probate expenses. I cannot make the arithmetic balance out, but this alone does not necessarily mean skullduggery, because it is obvious that many papers, previously lost or destroyed, had never been replaced, and may easily have explained whatever financial discrepancy existed. Slade's shares of Wells Fargo stock, $13,400.00, never came to light.

In any event, after the final settlement and the payment of all the approved bills there was $359.41 left for Mrs. Slade. Certain last expenses of closing the estate—which do not appear, except for an item of $36.00 paid to a newspaper April 16, 1866—were deducted from this. On October 27, 1866, the last money, $305.91, was paid over to Word & Spratt, attorneys for J. H. Kiskadden and M. V. Kiskadden. They likely paid this over to J. H. Kiskadden without knowing that his wife, the former Mrs. Slade, had already left him.

The historian can now determine that, while this estate was indeed administered, the Last Will and Testament of J. A. Slade never did show up, never was probated. The chroniclers who have asserted that his was the first will probated in Montana are in error.

On February 10, 1890, Mrs. Slade had a Chicago attorney, J. O'B. Scobey of 90 Washington St., Chicago, send a letter of inquiry about the estate. By this time typewriters were in use, and this letter is typed. On March 12, 1890, this attorney writes again on behalf of Mrs. Slade and he makes it clear that she was then destitue. (No record can be found in the National Archives that she had ever applied for a pension as a widow of a Mexican War veteran.) In neither letter does the attorney indicate that Mrs. Slade was claiming ownership of the Ravenswood ranch.

This failure of Mrs. Slade in 1890 to make any inquiry about the Ravenswood ranch can readily be explained by an event which took place in 1883. In that year Mrs. Slade, who must have been well along in middle age, returned to Virginia City and got married again, as we can see from the records of Madison County, Territory of Montana, Volume 6, page 379:

<table>
<tr><td>Marriage Certificate
Elhener Crosby
vs
Maria Slade</td><td>Territory of Montana
County of Madison</td></tr>
</table>

This is to certify that the undersigned Justice of the Peace in and for said County did on the 2nd day of April A.D. 1883 join in lawful wedlock Elhener Crosby and Maria Slade with their mutual consent in presence of Mrs. H Claston and Mrs J Mahan witnesses

M H Lott
Justice of the Peace

At that time she undoubtedly learned that ranch claims required continuous use and occupancy for their validity, that there were now such things as real property taxes, and that the Ravenswood land had been gobbled up by other settlers. If she had gone over the Virginia City hill to visit it, she would have found the greater portion in the possession of United States patentees Henry J. Sweet and Hein Kroger, U.S. Bureau of Land Management records, Billings, Montana.

Claims against the Estate

The claims against the estate, with regard to dates, names, amounts, etc., are approximately as follows: 3/9/64, O. R. Johnson, $39.00, not paid; 3/28/64, J. W. Todd, for boots, $67.80, paid in part?; 3/30/64, J. Hall & Co., bar bill, $50.50 or $55.55, paid by Adm.; 4/2/64, Johnson & Ferguson, $79.00, not paid; 4/18/64, Thompson & Hankins, bar bill, $101.00, not paid; 4/29/64, Virginia Hotel, meals and bar, $96.30, paid by Adm?; 6/15/64, lost claim of Kettle?; 6/22/64, John A. Creighton, whiskey & groceries, $120.54, paid by Est.; 7/5/64, J. W. Todd by Caleb P. Jones, business account, $53.00, paid in part?; 7/9/64, Idaho Billiard Room, liquor and breakage, $201.25, paid by Est.; 7/9/64, Wills & Brand, meals, loss of stool and broom $18.50, $14.00 paid by Est.; 7/9/64, Root and Davis, beans and vinegar, $32.00, paid by Est.; 7/11/64, F. Craine, labor on stone house, $216.00, not paid; 7/12/64, Jerry Nolan, whiskey, $23.80, not paid; 7/14/64, O'Dell, Wilkinson & Buckner, stable care, $123.00, paid by Est.

7/16/64, W. F. Bartlett, agent for J. J. Roe, clothing, $53.25, paid by Est.; 7/20/64, L. P. Crabtree, whiskey and cigars, $66.00, not paid, rejected; 7/25/64, Geo. B. Parker, store account, parts very old, $554.22, paid by Est.; 8/4/64, R. H. Sapp, 36 days as cattle man, $360.00, not paid; 8/19/64, Tufts, 30.00, Chumasero, 20.00, Sloan, 15.00, appraisers, $65.00, paid by Est.; 9/6/64, Geo. Higgins, for appraising ranches, $57.00, paid by Est.; 10/24/64, Geo. Parker, reimbursement for claims paid, $1503.25, paid by Est.; 11/19/64, Geo. J. Perkins, meals and bar bill, $38.25, paid by Est.; 12/27/64, Kettle, 77 pounds of pork, $57.75, paid by Est.; 12/31/64, Geo. Higgins, auctioning personal property, $17.67, paid by Est.; 1/13/65, James Williams, labor, $390.00, not paid; 1/13/65, James Boner, labor, $393.33, not paid; 1/?/65, Geo. Parker, revenue stamps, $5.00, paid by Est.; 4/7/65, Pfouts & Russell, whiskey & groceries, $165.00,—paid by Est.; 10/18/65, Kettle, copy of first claim for $57.75; 11/6/65, O'Dell, Wilkinson & Buckner, copy of first claim for $123.00; 11/8/65, Word & Spratt, attorney fees, $670.00, paid by Est.; plus whatever claims were lost and never replaced.

In considering the claims against the estate the layman should bear in mind that, generally speaking, anybody can put in a claim against a person's estate, but this doesn't necessarily mean that it will be paid; all claims must be investigated and approved by the administrator and the probate court before payment is authorized; and then the payment will be made only to the extent that money is available.

The claims against Slade's estate are numerous, indeed. They include lots of bar bills, approximately $500.00, plus whiskey purchases mixed in with grocery accounts. But the bigger part of the total is made up of what appears to be legitimate claims for household goods and business accounts. Many were rejected either by the administrator or the Probate Court. As stated before, no definite conclusions can be reached by checking things through with an adding machine, first, because several claims are missing, secondly, some claims were made in the name of a business firm at the outset but were evidently paid off to an individual agent of that firm, and at this time we can not make satisfactory identification between the two; and lastly, some claims may have been paid in reduced or increased amounts, so that we cannot confirm the identity of a particular claim by the exact amount paid. One thing cannot be disputed: Slade's credit was good.

There is nothing to show payment or reimbursement for the funeral service conducted at Virginia City by Rev. A. M. Torbet, (*Contributions to the Historical Society of Montana*, Vol. VI, p. 293.), or for the expense of burial and tombstone in Block B, Lot 6, Grave #7, in the Salt Lake City Cemetery, Utah. (See *Frontier Times*, May, 1976, p. 24.).

The claims picture brings up several questions of interest to the historian. One of these concerns a possible claim that never was in the estate file. In the Slade manuscript file at the museum library in Helena, Montana, there is a promissory note which is thought, and appears to me, to be an authentic item of Slade memorabilia.

This promissory note records a loan, September 24, 1863, by George Chrisman of $3460.00 to "Ely & Slade" to be repaid December 1, 1863. The signature, "Ely & Slade", is in one person's handwriting, without indicating which one. A comparison of the "Slade" part of the signature with the only authentic "Joseph A. Slade" signature that I have found, in the National Archives, is inconclusive; possibly a handwriting expert could give a definite yes or no about it. The reverse side of the note shows repayment of the $3460.00 at Virginia City, May 17, 1864, by Wilson & Co., this repayment without interest being acknowledged by George Chrisman through "Sanders." On that day, May 17, 1864, Slade's estate was in the process of being administered, yet Chrisman had filed no claim, and we find no record of any payment from the Slade estate on such a note. From this we can infer that the obligation of paying off the note was Ely's sole responsibility, and that Slade's name was on it merely as an accommodation maker. To me this tends strongly to prove that the promissory note is genuine. I think it can reasonably be theorized that the merchants of Bannack and Virginia City raised this money to finance Slade's freighting trip to Milk River, and that Chrisman had advanced the money on behalf of this group of merchants.

In my opinion the two most noteworthy claims are those of James Boner and James *H.* Williams. The identification of these two men cannot be made conclusively but we know from the Slade historians that the only James Boner ever connected with Slade was a former station tender for the Overland stage company in Wyoming; and the only James Williams ever connected with Slade was the man who became captain of the Vigilantes and was in charge of hanging Slade. If we assume that these are the identical men who filed these claims in Slade's estate, then we have a first rate curiosity for the scrutiny of any historian.

The estate file proves that on January 13, 1865, Boner and Williams went to Attorney Wilbur F. Sanders and had him prepare claims against Slade's estate on the theory that Boner and Williams were both personal employees of J. A. Slade. Boner swore that he had worked and labored for Slade from October 15, 1862, to July 25, 1863, at $40.00 per month for a total with interest of $393.33. Boner signed and swore to this claim before Wilbur F. Sanders. Williams endorsed Boner's claim, vouching for it as being true. Williams's own claim recited that he had worked for Slade from October 1, 1862, to January 1, 1863, at $30.00 per month ($90.00) and seven months, January 1, 1863, to August 15, 1863, at $40.00 per month ($300.00), for a total of $390.00 and interest. Williams signed and swore to this claim before Wilbur F. Sanders, and Boner endorsed it, vouching for the fact that Williams's claim was true. Both claims were filed with the Probate Court on January 26, 1865.

Wilbur F. Sanders then filed an undated paper in the Probate Court stating that these identical claims had been filed once before but had been lost or destroyed, and for that reason were made and filed again;

he then asked the Probate Court to compel Administrator Parker to pay these amounts to Boner and Williams.

Numerous western writers have recounted a story about how James Williams, later leader of the Vigilantes, had once accosted Slade and "faced him down" in a bloodless encounter of sheer nerve. It seems Williams and Slade were each leading wagon trains in the same direction, when they met and joined together for better protection against the Indians. Because of worry over Slade's drinking, the members of both wagons assembled to elect an overall wagon master, either Slade or Williams. Williams came to Slade, told him what was going on, and suggested that Slade join the assembly to look after his own interests in the election. Slade made a remark to the effect that it wouldn't matter how they voted; that he (Slade) would remain the leader. Williams thereupon contradicted Slade in a very hostile manner, saying that whoever was elected would be the leader—and nobody else. Whereupon Slade backed down on account of the threat in Williams's voice. In other words, J. A. Slade, whose name was feared on the frontier more than God Almighty, wilted down to nothing under the menace in James Williams's voice and aspect. Williams is quoted as telling people years later that as a consequence Slade was always well behaved in Williams's presence.

The only indication we have of when and where this incident took place is a news story in the *Alder Gulch Times* (Virginia City, Montana) of September 15, 1899: "Williams and Slade were old acquaintances. They first met at some point in Idaho on the old wagon road from Denver to this country, where a train had formed to come north. A captain was to be elected. Slade and Williams were the opposing candidates. . . ." If this newspaper story is true, it would indicate that this occurrence took place during the gold rush to Virginia City, that is, in May or June of 1863, Williams traveling over the Lander cut-off from the Pikes Peak area and Slade from Fort Bridger, with their meeting place somewhere near Soda Springs, Idaho. Judge Callaway stated flatly that the incident took place in June, 1863. There is no indication whatever when or with whom the story itself first originated —whether before or after Slade's death.

With these considerations in mind we must be bewildered by the fact that the Slade estate file proves that James Williams—not once, but twice—solemnly swore on his oath before Wilbur F. Sanders that at the time and place mentioned, and in this contested wagon-boss election, he was a personal employee of J. A. Slade, working for him at the rate of $40.00 per month!

So, too, with James Boner. In his interview with the editor of the

Alder Gulch Times, September 22, 1899—more than thirty-five years after Slade's death—Boner tells several anecdotes about Slade. He exhibits friendship and admiration for Slade, but in a long interview he never once mentioned that he ever worked for Slade personally. Old men forget many things, but they don't forget their various types of employment or whom they worked for. (At the time he tells about, when he nursed Slade back to health after Jules had shot him, they were both employees of the Overland stage company.). Yet, in 1864-65 Boner had joined twice with Williams in swearing an oath that he had been a personal employee of Slade's clear back to Virginia Dale days in Colorado!

Nowhere in the estate file can we find evidence that either Administrator Parker or the Probate Court ever approved the Williams and Boner claims; and the final accounts of Administrator Parker show affirmatively what creditors got what money. We must conclude from these undisputed court records that neither Williams nor Boner got a dime. Also, lawyers will agree (?) that under all the facts—the solvency of the Slade estate, the payment of all legitimate claims, and the fact that these two claimants were represented by very competent counsel, Wilbur F. Sanders—the Administrator and the Probate Court must have faced some very compelling reasons forcing them to take the position that the claims of Williams and Boner were false.

In concluding these remarks about the claims picture it should be said that one of the sad things that the examiner of the Slade estate file will come upon are a few claims for bar bills and liquor, appearing to run right up to, and including, the day of his death. Historians generally agree that Slade had been whooping it up for several days previously, but these few claims give us documentary evidence tending to corroborate the truth of a direct quotation attributed to Wilbur F. Sanders that immediately before the hanging Slade was "still drunk." (*Fifteen Thousand Miles by Stage*, Carrie Adell Strahorn, 1911, p. 108)

What if Mrs. Slade had stayed on in Virginia City and managed the estate business herself? She could have done this even though Slade's last will and testament might have been lost. As his surviving widow she still had the first right to be appointed administratrix.

To me it seems very clear that, if Mrs. Slade had toughed it out on the spot, the final result of these probate proceedings would have been very different. At least half of the creditors would never have filed a claim against her; and the other half would have hesitated considerably before attempting to enforce collection. The two ranch properties would never have been sold, and her interest in the "Slade and Jones" mine would have paid off on its true value.

The early miners of Virginia City were quick to rise up in anger and hang a man but they would have been equally quick to rise up in sympathy to protect his widow in the full enjoyment of all her husband's property. Mrs. Slade was a courageous and resourceful woman. With the Indian boy Jimmy to help, with the extensive personal property and the excellent ranch land at her disposal, she could have lived well and prospered. Last but not least, she would have been on hand to spike most of the slanderous yarns and folklorian nonsense which sprang up to blacken the name of Joseph A. Slade.

Bibliography

Books and Magazines

Abbott, Newton Carl. *Montana in the Making*. Billings, Montana: Gazette Printing Company, 1943.

Adams, Ramon F., comp. *Six Guns and Saddle Leather*. Rev. ed., Norman, Oklahoma: University of Oklahoma Press, 1969.

Bancroft, Hubert Howe. *The Works of Hubert Howe Bancroft*, 39 vols. San Francisco: The History Company, Publishers, 1883-1890.

Beebe, Lucius, and Clegg, Charles. *U. S. West*. New York: E. P. Dutton & Co., Inc., 1949.

Biedler, X. X. *Biedler, Vigilante*. Ed. by Helen Fitzgerald Sanders with William H. Bertsche, Jr. Norman, Oklahoma: University of Oklahoma Press, 1957.

Birney, Hoffman. *Vigilantes*. Philadelphia: The Penn Publishing Co., 1929.

Boren, Kerry Ross. "Jack Slade's Grave Located." *Frontier Times* magazine, April-May, 1976.

Bruffey, George A. *Eighty-one Years in the West*. Butte, Montana: The Butte Miner Company, 1925.

Callaway, Llewellyn Link. *Two True Tales of the Wild West*. Oakland, California: Maud Gonne Press, 1973.

Callaway, Lew L. "Joseph Alfred Slade: Killer or Victim" *Montana Magazine of History*, January, 1953 p. 5.

Chadwick, George C. "Wells Fargo Colts." *Gun Report* magazine, December, 1957, p. 15.

Chapman, Arthur. *The Pony Express*. New York and London: G. P. Putnam's Sons, 1932.

__________. "Jack Slade, Mankiller." Undated, unidentified magazine. Slade file. Montana Historical Society library, Helena, Montana.

__________. "Slade of the Overland." *Union Pacific Magazine*, January, 1931.

__________. "Vigilante Vengeance." *Elks Magazine*, August, 1927.

Clayton, William. *The Latter-Day Saints' Emigrants' Guide: . . . From Council Bluffs to the Valley of the Great Salt Lake*. St. Louis: Mo. Republican Steam Power Press, Chambers & Knapp, 1848.

Collins, Dabney Otis. *The Hanging of Bad Jack Slade*. Denver, Colorado: Golden Bell Press, 1963.

Colyer, Julie Beehrer. "Freighting Across the Plains." *Montana Magazine of Western History*, Vol. XII, No. 4, 1962, p. 2.

Coutant, Charles Griffin. *History of Wyoming*. Laramie, Wyoming: 1899.

Cram, George F. *Cram's Unrivalled Family Atlas of the World, Indexed*. Chicago: Donohue & Henneberry, 1897.

Crawford, Lewis F. *Rekindling Camp Fires*:The Exploits of Ben Arnold (Connor). Bismarck, N.D.: Capitol Book Co., 1926.

Davis, Jean. *Shallow Diggins*. Caldwell, Idaho: Caxton Printers, Ltd., 1963.

DeVoto, Bernard. *Across the Wide Missouri*. New York: Bonanza Books, 1947.

Dimsdale, Thomas J. *Vigilantes of Montana*, 12th ed. Butte, Montana: McKee Printing Co., 1950.

Driggs, Howard R. *The Pony Express Goes Through*. New York and Philadelphia: J. B. Lippincott Company, 1963.

Eberhardt, Perry. *Treasure Tales of the Rockies*. Chicago: Sage Books, 1961.

Fisher, Vardis, and Holmes, Opal Laurel. *Gold Rushes and Mining Camps*. Caldwell, Idaho: The Caxton Printers, Ltd., 1968.

Frederick, J. V. *Ben Holladay, the Stagecoach King*. Glendale, California: The Arthur H. Clark Co., 1940.

Guldbeck, Per E. *The Care of Historical Collections*. Nashville, Tennessee: American Association for State and Local History, 1972.

Hafen, LeRoy R., Hollen, W. Eugene and Rister, Carl Coke. *Western America*, 3rd ed., Englewood Cliffs, New Jersey: Prentice Hall, Inc., 1970.

Hansen, Harry, ed. *Colorado, A Guide to the Highest State*. New York: Hastings House, 1970.

Haven, Charles T. and Belden, Frank A. *History of the Colt Revolver*. New York: Bonanza Books, 1940.

Hebard, Grace Raymond and Brininstool, E. A. *The Bozeman Trail*, 2 vols. Cleveland: The Arthur H. Clark Company, 1922.

Hicks, John D. and Mowry, George E. *Short History of American Democracy*. Boston: Houghton Mifflin Company, 1956.

Hough, Emerson. *Story of the Outlaw*. New York: The Outing Publishing Co., 1907.

Hungerford, Edward. *Wells Fargo*. New York: Random House, 1949.

Hutchens, John K. *One Man's Montana*. Philadelphia & New York: J. B. Lippincott Company, 1964.

Inman, Henry and Cody, William F. *Great Salt Lake Trail*. New York: The Macmillan Co., 1898. Topeka, Kansas: reprint, 1914.

Johnson, Dorothy M. *Western Badmen*. New York: Dodd, Mead, 1970.

Langford, Nathaniel Pitt. *Vigilante Days and Ways*. Chicago: A. C. McClurg & Co., 1923.

Lederer, Paul S. "How the Navy Drifted Into Buying Navies." *The American Rifleman*. March, 1973, p. 30.

Leeson, M. A. *History of Montana, 1739-1885*. Chicago: 1885.

Loomis, Noel M. *Wells Fargo*. New York: Bramhall House, 1968.

Madison County History Association. *Pioneer Trails and Trials*. Great Falls, Montana: Blue Print & Letter Company, 1976.

Majors, Alexander. *Seventy Years on the Frontier*. Minneapolis: Ross & Haines, Inc., 1965.

Marquis, Thomas B. *Memoirs of a White Crow Indian: Thomas H. Leforge*. Lincoln, Nebraska: University of Nebraska Press, 1974.

Miller, Joaquin. *An Illustrated History of Montana*. Chicago: 1894.

Mockel, Myrtle. *Montana*. Chicago: Sage Books, 1969.

Monaghan, Jay, ed., *Book of the American West*. New York: Bonanza Books, 1963.

Montana Historical Society. *Contributions*. Vols. I to X, 1876-1940. Reprint, 1966.

————. *Montana the Magazine of Western History*.

————. Comp. & ed. *Not In Precious Metals Alone*. Helena, Montana: Montana Historical Society Press, 1976.

Moody, Ralph. *The Old Trails West*. Promontory Press, 1963.

Morton, Julius Sterling. *History of Nebraska*. Lincoln, Nebraska: 1906-1907.

Muir, Florabel. "Hanged for a Song." *Liberty* magazine, June 30, 1928.

Ovitt, Mable. *Golden Treasure*. Caldwell, Idaho: Caxton Printers, Ltd., 1952.

Parkhill, Forbes. *The Law Goes West*. Denver: Sage Books, 1956.

Peltier, Jerome, ed. & comp. *Banditti of the Rocky Mountains*. Minneapolis: Ross & Haines, Inc., 1964.

Progressive Men of the State of Montana. Chicago: A. W. Bowen & Co., (n.d.), circa 1902.

Prophet, Don. *The Saga of Slade*. New York: Pageant Press, Inc., 1958.

Quiett, Glenn Chesney. *Pay Dirt*. New York: D. Appleton-Century Co., 1936.

Reinhardt, Richard. *Out West on the Overland Train*. Palo Alto, California: American West Publishing Company, 1967.

Richardson, James D. ed. & comp. *Messages and Papers of the Presidents*, 20 vols. New York: Bureau of National Literature, Inc., 1897.

Root, Frank A. and Connelley, William E. *The Overland Stage to California—The Pony Express*. Topeka, Kansas: 1901. Reprint ed., Glorieta, New Mexico: Rio Grande Press, Inc., 1970.

Rosa, Joseph G. *The Gunfighter—Man or Myth?* Norman, Oklahoma: University of Oklahoma Press, 1969.

Russel, Edward C., ed. *Proceedings of the Montana Bar Association*. Vol. I. Helena, Montana: State Publishing Company, 1902.

Sabin, Edwin L. *Wild Men of the Wild West*. New York: Thomas Y. Crowell Company, 1929.

Sanders, Helen Fitzgerald. *A History of Montana*. 3 vols. Chicago and New York: The Lewis Publishing Company, 1913.

Sanders, James U., ed. *Society of Montana Pioneers*, Vol. 1. Akron, Ohio: The Werner Company, 1899.

Serven, James E. *Colt Firearms*. Santa Ana, California: The Foundation Press, 1954.

Settle, Mary Lund and Raymond W. *Saddles and Spurs*. New York: Bonanza Books, 1955.

Shumaker, P. L. *Colt's Variations of the Old Model Pocket Pistol*. Alhambra, California: Borden Publishing Company, 1957.

Smith, Justin Harvey. *The War with Mexico*. New York: The McMillan Company, 1919.

Stout, Tom, ed. *Montana, Its Story and Biography*. 3 vols. Chicago and New York: The American Historical Society, 1921.

Strahorn, Carrie Adell. *Fifteen Thousand Miles by Stage*. New York and London: G. P. Putnam's sons, 1911, 1915.

Stewart, George R. "Travelers by 'Overland'." *The American West*, Vol. V, No. 4, July, 1968.

Stuart, Granville. *Forty Years on the Frontier*. 2 vols. Cleveland: The Arthur H. Clark Company, 1925.

Toponce, Alexander. *Reminiscences of Alexander Toponce*. Norman, Oklahoma: University of Oklahoma Press, 1971.

Trenholm, Virginia Cole. *Footprints on the Frontier*. Douglas, Wyoming: Douglas Enterprise Co., 1945.

__________. "Save Sibley". *Montana Magazine of Western History*. Vol. XII, No. 4, 1962.

Twain, Mark. *Roughing It*. New York and London: Harper & Brothers, 1913.

Van Zandt, Franklin K. *Boundaries of the United States and the Several States*. Geological Survey Bulletin 1212. Washington: United States Government Printing Office, 1966.

Vestal, Stanley. *Jim Bridger*. West Caldwell, N.J.: William Morrow & Co., 1946.

Walker, Henry Pickering. *The Wagonmasters.* Norman, Oklahoma: University of Oklahoma Press, 1966.

Ware, Eugene F. *The Indian War of 1864.* Lincoln, Nebraska: University of Nebraska Press, 1960.

Watrous, Ansel. *History of Larimer County, Colorado.* Fort Collins, Colorado: The Courier Printing & Publishing Co., 1911.

Wilson, R. L. *The Arms Collection of Colonel Colt.* Bullville, New York: Herb Glass, 1964.

Works Progress Administration. *Utah, A Guide to the State.* 1940.

Young, Rowland L. "Where the Deer and the Antelope Play." *American Bar Association Journal*, 57, June, 1971: 577-579.

Encyclopedias

American Peoples Encyclopedia. 1969, s.v. "Jim Bridger" by Frederick E. Voelker.

Dictionary of American Biography. 1935 ed., s.v. "Slade, Joseph Alfred".

Newspapers

Interview with James Boner. *Alder Gulch Times*, Virginia City, Montana. 15 and 22 September 1899.

Interview with Charles Higganbotham. *The Anaconda Standard*, Butte, Montana. June 20, 1920, Part II, p. 1.

Commonwealth, Denver, November 13, 1862.

Interview with Robert P. Menefee. *The Madisonian.* Virginia City, Montana, September 1, 1899.

"Ninety Years of Controversy Started with Hanging of Joseph A. Slade," Warren N. Reichman. *The Madisonian*, Virginia City, Montana, May 29, 1953.

Miners Register, Denver, November 14, 1862.

Records

National Archives, Washington, D.C.

Official records, and Court files of Madison County, Virginia City, Montana.

Index

Albuquerque 39
Alder Gulch 28, 33
Alder Gulch Times 61, 62
Alton, Illinois 38-40
Amon Carter Museum 24
Angel's Camp 19
Arizona 17, 40
Auburn 19

Bannack, 28, 29, 56, 60
Bartlett, W.F. 58
Baume, Thomas 50-53
Beam, J. W. 52
Beni, Jules 15, 62
Benicia 19
Billings, Montana 50, 58
Bissel, Dr. G.G. 45
Bitter Creek 34
Blake, Henry N. 45
Board of County Supervisors 19, 20
Bond, Captain Thomas 38-39
Boner, James 23, 26, 29, 56, 59, 60-62
Bowman, Richard G. 34-35
Bridger, Jim 17, 26
Bridger Pass 15
Brown, W.W. 54-55
Bureau of Land Management 43, 50, 58
Burnt Ranch 26

Calaveras County 42
California 17, 20, 24, 33, 39-43
California, Census, 1850 42
California Gold Country 11, 17
Callaway, Judge 25, 28, 43, 61
Carlyle, Illinois 15, 37, 40-42
Cedar Spring 38
Chapman, Arthur 28
Chapultepec 37, 39
Chicago, Illinois 38
Chrisman, George 59-60
Civil War 11
Claston, Mrs. H. 58
Clinton County 40
Cold Spring 38
Coloma 17
Colorado 13, 15, 17, 33-35, 40, 47, 62
Colt revolver 11, 15, 21

Compromise of 1850 15, 17
Comstock 17
Continental Divide 15, 17, 26-27, 34
Cook and Campbell 47-48
Crabtree, L. P. 58
Craine, F. 58
Creighton & Co. 54-55
Creighton, John A. 50, 58
Christenot, Benjamin F. 55
Crosby, Elhener (?) 57-58
Chumasero 58

Dakota 17
Davis, Judge 20
Deming, Elias P. 41
Denver 15, 33
Denver Republican newspaper 28
Depot 43, 17, 19
Depot, stage 18-20
Domis, M. 53

Echo, Utah 31
Edgar, Henry 28, 45
Eldorado County 11, 17-20, 42
Eldorado County records 20
El Paso 39
Ely & Slade 59
Ennis, Montana 49-50

Farson, Wyoming 33
Fort Benton 34
Fort Bridger 15, 17, 19-20, 26-29, 33-34,
    61
Fort Collins 35
Fort Hall 29
Fort Halleck 26, 29
Fort Leavenworth 38
Fort Sumter 11

Gettysburg Museum 20, 31
Gilbert, Henry S. 27-29
Gilbert, Mrs. 29
Gilbert's Trading Post 26
Gilbert, William H. 29
Granite Gulch mining district 53
Green River 27-28, 33
Griffith & Thompson 54-55

72   *Index*

Hall, Amos C. 51
Hall, Chief Justice 29
Hall, J. & Co. 58
Hall, J. J. 56
Ham's Fork 27-28, 33
Hangtown 17
Higginbotham, Charles 24
Higgins, Geo. 56, 58
Higgins & Thorne 54-55
Holladay, Ben. 15, 24
Honorable Discharge 39-40
Howie, Neil, deputy sheriff 49, 55

Idaho 17, 33, 50
Idaho Billiard Room 58
Illinois 37
Illinois Foot Volunteers, First Regiment 37-39

Jackson, J. Q. 19
Jimmy, Indian boy 47, 63
Johnson & Ferguson 58
Johnson, O. R. 58
Johnston, Gen. Albert Sidney 26
Jones, Caleb P. 58
Jones, T. C., probate judge 33, 49, 50-53
Jones, Thomas 51-53
Joslyn rifle 20, 31
Julesburg Museum 29, 31

Kalispell, Montana 35
Kansas 17, 33
Kettle, G. E. 56, 58-59
Kiskadden 56-57
Kroger, Hein 58

Lake, C. G. 19
Lander's Cut Off 26-27, 61
Langford, Nathaniel Pitt 28
Las Vegas, New Mexico 39
Limetad 38
Lone Tree claim 53
Loomis, Noel M. 15, 18-20, 22, 35
Lott, M. H. 51-52, 58
Louisiana Purchase 40
Love, Paul H. 45
Lower Cimerone Spring 38
Lower Rio Del Norte 39
Lutts, W.N. 51

Madison River district 46
Madison Valley 28, 50

Mahan, Mrs. J. 58
Maillet, Louis R. 23, 28
Majors, Alexander 39
Mansfield, W.H. 19
Mariposa County 42
Mason, E. C. 50
McAllister, Montana 50
McCarty, Lea Franklin 31
Menefee, Robert P. 30
Mexican War 15, 37-38, 40, 57
Mexico 37-38
Mexico City 39
Middaugh, Jas. L. 51
Milk River 28, 60
Mill Bar 53
Miners Gulch Government 45-46, 49, 51
Mississippi 17
Molino del Rey, battle 39
Monida Pass 29
Montana 13, 33, 46-47, 51, 56
Montana Historical Society 20, 45
Montana vigilantes 14, 48, 60-61
Mormon Boy claim 53
Morris, Thomas 51
Mullan, Captain John 34
Murieta, Joaquin 43

Neasham, Irene Simpson 13, 23
Nebraska 17, 33, 47
Nevada 17, 33, 40
Nevada mining district 49, 51
New Mexico 17, 39-41
Newby, Colonel Edward W. B. 38
Nighwander, J. W. 51-52
Nolan, Jerry 58
Norris, W. J. 54-55
North Dakota 33

Oath of Identity 40
O'Dell, Wilkinson & Buckner 58-59
Oregon 17, 33
Parker, George B. 20, 32, 48-59, 61-62
Parkhill, Forbes 29
Perkins, George J. 58
Pfouts & Russell 59
Phillips, Thomas F. 50
Pikes Peak 61
Pioneer museum 35
Placerville 17, 19-20
Pony Express 15, 18, 25, 39
Potter, M. W. 31

Puebla, seige of 39
Pulvidera 39

Ravenswood 46, 49-50, 55-58
Reni, Jules (seen Beni)
Rockfellow, John S. 55
Rocky Mountains 17, 27
Rocky Ridge 25
Roe, J. J. 58
Root & Davis 58
Root, J. J. Co., 54-55
Rosenstock, Fred A. 28
Russell, Charles M. 23, 28

Sacramento 42-43
Sacramento County 42
Salt Lake 33, 35, 48-49
Salt Lake grave 59
Sanders, Wilbur F. 30, 32, 46-47, 52, 56, 60-62
San Phillippe, New Mexico 39
Santa Fe, New Mexico 38
Santa Fe trail 38, 39
Sapp, R. H. 58
Scobey, J. O'B. 57
Scott, General 39
Secora, New Mexico 38
Sheriff of Eldorado County 19
Shirley & Co. 19
Slade, A. J. 53
Slade & Jones claims 51, 53, 62
Slade, E. B. 42
Slade, Edward G. 42
Slade, Geo. D. 42
Slade, Geo. W. 42
Slade Gulch 28
Slade, Isac 42
Slade, J. 14-15
Slade, Jas. B. 42
Slade, J. B. 42
Slade, Jeremiah 42
Slade, Jno. W. 42
Slade, John M. 42
Slade, Maria Virginia 15, 31-32, 46-52, 54-55, 57-58, 62-63
Slade ,Thos. P. 42
Slade, Wm. 42
Slade's claim 50
Sleeper 21-22
Sloan 58

Slode, J. 13, 15, 19-20, 35
Smith, Hon. Robert 41-42
Socorro 38-39
Soda Springs 29, 33, 61
South Dakota 33
Southmady, C. W. 50-53
Southmayd, Leroy 50-51, 53
Southmayd, S. and Co. 51
South Pass 17, 25-26
South Pass Stage Station 26
Spotswood, Robert 23, 29
Spring Dale 46, 50, 55-56
St. Joe 17
Stuart, Granville 28
Stuart, Mrs. Granville 32
Sweet, Henry J. 58
Sweetwater 26

Tahoe, Lake 17
Texas 17, 37, 40
Thompson & Hankins 58
Todd, J. W. 58
Todd, Richard 45
Torbet, Rev. A. M. 59
Tufts 58

Upper Sweetwater Pony Express Station 26
Utah 13, 17, 33, 40

Vigilantes 25, 30, 48, 60-61
Virginia City, Montana 15, 17, 28-30, 33, 40, 49, 51-53, 55-63
Virginia City, Nevada 17
Virginia Dale 15, 17, 29, 35, 62
Virginia Hotel 58

Walla Walla, Washington 34
Washington, D. C. 41
Washington Territory 13, 15, 17, 19, 27, 33-34
Wells Fargo & Co. 13, 15, 17-22, 24, 34-35, 43, 57
Wells Fargo Bank History Room 13, 23
West and Dickason 51
Whetstone Springs 38
Williams, James 28, 56, 59-62
Wills & Brand 58
Wilson & Co. 60
Word & Spratt, attorneys 57, 59
Wyoming 13, 15, 17, 31, 33, 40, 47